TODAY'S INSPIRED *Young* LATINA

VOLUME III

INSPIRATION FROM YOUNG PROFESSIONAL LATINAS PURSUING THEIR DREAMS

Jacqueline S. Ruiz

Alexandria Rios Taylor

TODAY'S INSPIRED YOUNG LATINA

This book is a compilation of stories from numerous people who have each contributed a chapter and is designed to provide inspiration to our readers.

It is sold with the understanding that the publisher and the individual authors are not engaged in the rendering of psychological, legal, accounting or other professional advice. The content and views in each chapter are the sole expression and opinion of its author and not necessarily the views of Fig Factor Media, LLC.

For more information, contact:

Jacqueline S. Ruiz
Fig Factor Media, LLC | www.figfactormedia.com
JJR Marketing, Inc. | www.jjrmarketing.com

Cover Design & Layout by Juan Pablo Ruiz
Printed in the United States of America

FIG
FACTOR
MEDIA

ISBN: 978-1-952779-85-5

Library of Congress Number: 2020943290

To our families,
Thank you for making the impossible
possible.

Table of Contents:

Acknowledgements

This book would not have been possible without the contributions of many. First, we would like to thank the young Latinas who have contributed to this project and the others still embarking on their journeys. Their goals and steady determination have continued to be a constant source of inspiration for us all, and it has shown us that our work must push on.

We also want to thank Elizabeth Colón for her contribution to this project and for sharing her journey with us in the preface. We are so grateful to influential mentors like her who have helped make this project a success.

Finally, We'd like to thank our editor, Shannon Mages, our author concierge, Gaby Hernández-Franch, our content specialist, Natalie Citro, and the entire design team. Their contributions have brought these stories to life, and their support has helped us make *Today's Young Inspired Latina* an inspiration for others.

Introduction

When we first published *Today's Inspired Young Latina,* we never imagined the magic we would have been able to create. Through this project, we have reached 50 young Latinas and watched as they have transformed themselves into authors and catapulted their lives for success. It has been an honor to watch as they courageously share their stories of strength, victory, and triumph, and find their communities of support.

This project was first born out of a desire to help other young Latina women find their voice and create a space of representation. We hope that these stories of transformational success help inspire all of the young girls today looking for themselves within the media. Ensuring our youth have positive representation reflected in their literature has always been a goal close to our hearts and the continuation of this project. Too often, we see that the literature young Latinas have access to only shares a deficit model of representation, often highlighting low literacy rates and poverty in the home. Unfortunately, this does not provide a strong sense of self-agency for the young Latinas that need it most. We hope that by providing a means for an alternative narrative, we can help illuminate all of the fantastic things these strong Latina women can accomplish, thus, allowing others to view this anthology as a pathway of power and beauty.

With the first two editions of *Today's Inspired Young Latina,* it quickly became apparent just how powerful these young women's narratives were. The goal to continue sharing their stories became clear. We have continued to receive positive feedback on the project not only from peers but in the form of awards. Nominated as the Most Inspirational Young Adult Book through the International Book Awards, *Today's Inspired Young Latina* continued to provide us with signs that our work must go on. The successes of the first two editions of *Today's Inspired Young Latina* paved our path to push forward with a sense of duty to continue our work and a calling to help others transform through the process of writing.

For this third edition to the anthology, you will find that we pushed beyond the greater Chicago area with most of our young Latinas, living across The United States; we feel this has helped us to represent Latinas of various backgrounds more completely. Most of our young authors have also had the opportunity to share their stories in the Young LATINATalks. While they already understand the importance of sharing their journey on stage, now they have the opportunity to do so through writing. We have turned our focus for this edition to highlight the continued evolution of success and the transformational journeys we embark on along the way. We believe that most importantly, you will come to understand the journey to accomplish your goals through the stories of these young Latinas!

We have been so inspired by how these young women have bravely taken on the title of author to share their stories not only with their family and community—but also with the world. We have been honored to work alongside these women and watch as they bravely transformed from community members to community leaders. As you read along with the stories in this anthology, you will see themes of resilience, forgiveness, dedication, and perseverance come to life.

Our goal has been to use our platform to share the success of others, but we have recognized that sharing one's story of success is about more than what they were able to accomplish. It is also about the unexpected trials they face along the way and how they come to overcome such obstacles. These difficult times have transformed our young authors into the powerful forces they continue to be. They allow their lights to shine not only through their successes, but the telling of their journeys. Their stories help us to understand how the power of love, loss, relocation, and immigration becomes a uniting force for other young Latinas worldwide to find strength and create transformational journeys full of victory, hope, belief, and power.

We know that these young authors will become powerful forces within the Latina community, and we cannot wait to see what they go on to achieve. We hope that these stories of triumph and victory during times of transition serve as your reminder of the potential you hold within yourself to accomplish your goals. If you are reading these stories feeling like you have yet to achieve your goals, we hope you finish this anthology with a sense that the impossible is always possible. We believe in you, and we are here cheering you on along the journey to success!

Love,

Alex and Jackie

Preface

BY ELIZABETH COLÓN

CEO of Metaphrasis Language and Cultural Solutions, LLC.

Sharing your story is extremely important. Being able to step up and open yourself up to share is amazing. However, doing so hasn't always been as accessible as it is today. Growing up, it wasn't common to have both the ability and access to share your story with the world. But today, for young Latinas to have the platform to be able to step up and say, "I want to share my story with the world," is a gift to the next generation and others who may be confronting the same issues in their own lives.

When I was first asked to contribute to *Today's Inspired Young Latina*, it brought me back to my childhood. I often think about what it was like growing up, the lonely journey both my siblings and I had to embark on. Growing up in a home with a single mother raising six other children and a father who was an alcoholic, we had no one else to turn to except one another. Our childhood often trained us not to share with others the struggles we were enduring.

These shared familial experiences led us to falsely believe not having access to a voice was common for others. In our household, we weren't allowed to share. We couldn't seek help for my mother because she didn't want anybody to know about her suffering. These shared experiences ultimately caused us to grow up with little confidence and low self-esteem. We didn't get to speak up. We didn't get to share our struggles. Instead, we all seemed to share an overwhelming sense that we did not belong.

We struggled to believe in all of the things we had to offer the world. It truly made us question who we were, what we should be able to strive for, and what we could accomplish. We found ourselves asking: "Were we even college-worthy?" or "Were we individuals of a single mother who had to repeat the path that she was on?" "Do I go to college, or do I just get married and have children?"

All of these internal debates start to add up, and it got to a point in my life where I was beginning to question everything I did and the person I was becoming. I would stand in the mirror asking myself crucial questions like: "Who am I?" "What do I want to accomplish?" "Do I show up as I am, or do I be something or someone that maybe society wants me to be?"

When I think back to when I was a young girl, I was quite a little rebel for my family. At times, I held a lot of resentment, so I was always getting myself into trouble one way or another. I didn't believe college was for me. I did want to go to college, but my counselor said no, and did not recommend it. He said I was not worthy, so I believed him and threw that idea behind me. Instead, I got married at eighteen, and I really struggled to believe in myself at that point in my life.

When I decided to turn my life around, it was a little bit late in the game. In my late thirties, I decided I did not want to continue to live the life that I was living. If I continued down this path, I knew my future was in danger. I thought to myself, is this really the life I wanted to be living twenty years from now? The reality was that it wasn't. So, I took the necessary steps to turn my life in a new direction. I got out of my unhealthy relationship. I quit my job. I stepped up and put everything I had into the business that I have created today. I took a chance on myself!

It was a lonely journey because I didn't have mentors or anyone to tell me that I could do this, but I believed in myself. I told myself I was going to make this work. I had reached a point in my life where I knew I had to do that for myself because no one else was going to be doing it for me. Everything that I did, every step that I took, always came down to me talking to myself, telling myself that I could make this work. That I was going to be okay and that I was making the right decisions. I am happy that I am at a place in life where I can give back and help others take a more empowering route, and assist them in their business endeavors. Today I am proud to say I am the first Latina president of NAWBO Chicago, the largest chapter in the United States of the National Association of Women Business Owners.

The reality is that sometimes minority communities, in general, are often labeled in a certain way or by specific categories when it comes to education and levels of success. Depending on your situation, becoming self-sufficient, getting a higher-education degree, or becoming an entrepreneur is sometimes far-fetched. While it isn't always what society expects from us, if we can overcome those barriers and say, "I'm worthy! I can do this!" that's a huge accomplishment for all of us as a collective. These declarations are precisely the type that the incredible young women from *Today's Inspired Young Latina* are using to share their narratives. For these young Latinas to want to share the important parts of their lives and their journey on paper is an important first step to becoming who they are.

My advice to all of the other young Latinas feeling like you don't have someone who encourages or pushes you into becoming the best version of yourself is to be that person! While it may be difficult at times, it is vital to believe that the person you are becoming is the best version of yourself, and that nothing is impossible for you! You're going to have to believe in yourself to push towards your goals. I know firsthand just how difficult that can be, but at times being our own biggest fan is exactly how we find the courage to accomplish incredible things. I believe that we have to continue to encourage each other to quiet the noise around us and begin creating mantras and core beliefs that we can go back to every single day. Because ultimately, taking the time every day to repeat such strengths to yourself helps inspire courage. That's important.

The journey is not easy. It comes with lots of struggles, but it's just an opportunity to learn something else and grow from it. Each opportunity and struggle, take it with you. Keep it in your pocket. Remember it for the next adventure that you embark on. You are special and important, and the world is ready for you!

Elizabeth Colón

CEO of Metaphrasis Language and Cultural Solutions, LLC.

President of NAWBO Chicago Chapter

Young Latina Stories

THE SCARS OF CHOOSING YOURSELF

YASMIN AMARO-GARCIA

"It is not the end. It can't be."

My life has not been simple or average, but it is commonly uncommon. Growing up as a Mexican American female, there was immense pressure and a number of responsibilities I had as the eldest daughter. I was expected to be an excellent student, a caregiver to my sisters and behave properly. As I got older, these responsibilities started taking a toll on my mental health because, on top of all of these tasks, I was trying to accomplish something else.

As a result of this mounting pressure, the only places I found comfort were numbers. My grade point average and the number on my scale were the driving sources of my self-esteem, as dictated by the worth my mother put on them. The higher my grades were and the lower my weight was, the better I felt with myself because I was getting closer to maybe one day reaching my mother's approval and love.

I was deteriorating inside and out. I was doing all of these things, but I did not have permission to socialize with others outside of school often, to be able to love the person of my choosing openly, or to simply have a day where everything I did wasn't being criticized. I was not allowed to be free in the nation of symbolic freedom. I could not do it anymore. I could not be "perfect" anymore, it was costing me everything. Every part of me.

SPOKEN FREEDOM

A month after I turned 20, I approached my mother to let her know that I was sleeping over at my girlfriend's house after a school dance. Just like all my previous attempts to be independent, she said no. My mother, as usual, told me that I was setting a horrible example for my sisters. That, along with my attitude, I will never become a nurse. That I was being dramatic about wanting my own "freedom" and that I did not contribute anything to my family deemed worthy of having a sleepover.

Tears streaming down my face and my voice cracking, I replied, "I provide for this family way more than you do. I cook. I clean. I take you and my sisters everywhere you need to go. I arrange my schedule to accommodate your every need, on top of going to college. I do all of this on my own with no help from you. How could you not see that your daughters are deteriorating right in front of you? I have a freaking eating disorder because of you!"

My stepdad shifts in their bed as the noise makes it difficult for him to sleep for his next day of work. My mother looks at him and shakes her head when she responds, "You're wrong, this is the first I am hearing of your 'eating disorder.' If you really had an eating disorder, just go eat the food in the kitchen; we have enough! You just put things in your head and everyone else's head for your sake, you need help. All of you need help, I don't need it."

My mind began spinning with the words she said over and over again for twenty years, two decades of the same words in different time frames, two decades of my life of obedience, with mental breakdowns labeled as insanity as I scratched my way up to the surface for air. I spat back, *"Madre no eres." You are no mother.*

I stormed out of her room, found my shoes, and walked out into the cold, midnight air. I walked to the community park and sat on one of the swings, pulled my phone out, and called my girlfriend to summarize what had happened. I tell her I'm okay, that I'll figure it out.

I looked out onto the road and broke down in hysterical sobs. My second panic attack of the month. I ask myself, Why do I have to keep going through this? Why am I not enough? I watch the cars racing in different directions. *What if I just...?*

My body started getting up. NO! I screamed to myself. You have so much more to say to do. It is not the end. It can't be.

BREAKING FREE

The winter air forced me back home in the early morning. I woke up in my bed with my head weighing my body down, feeling defeated as my attempt to sleep out in the wild had failed. I got ready for the school day and to drop off my mom at one of her many errands. We drove in silence, neither one of us saying a word until we reached her destination, and she slammed the door.

As soon as I was out of her sight, I began to feel the panic and hysteria of another panic attack, as I lost feeling in my legs and arms. I continued to drive to school. Throughout the years, I sporadically had panic attacks, but recently, as I tried to advocate for myself, panic attacks became a weekly occurrence.

I went through my scheduled motions of attending class, tutoring, and arrived right on time for my meeting with the Director of TRIO-Student Support Services (TRIO-SSS) to discuss how my semester was going. I am required to meet with my designated TRIO-SSS advisor every semester as I am part of a first-generation college student organization aiming to help students complete their degrees successfully. As I was applying for a public speaking event which she was best informed on, I decided to meet with her instead.

"So, Yasmin, tell me what's going on, how is everything at home?" she asked.

I wanted to lie, I wanted to tell her everything was okay; I've done it a million times to a million different faces. I wanted to protect my mother, but I couldn't. I had given my everything and lost myself. So, I told her what happened last night with tears streaming down my neck into my pink hoodie.

In between panic attacks, she held me close and said words I will never forget, "You're not going back there, okay? We will figure this out because you can't keep doing this. As someone who went through something similar, I am telling you that this could get much worse. So, let me make some calls and tell your girlfriend where to find you because you are not going home."

Dozens of thoughts raced through my mind: *Oh god, why did I say anything? What will my mom think? This is insane, I can't leave. This isn't the plan. I never wanted to leave until it was time to take my sisters with me.*

Reading my face of panic, she said, "Honey, I know you want to protect your sisters and be there for them. I know that this is who you have been. If you really want to help them, you have to take care of yourself and show them that it is possible to get out of that. You are of no help to them if you are actively deteriorating in their presence." It was time; it was time for me.

Later that day as I attended a presentation, I received an email from the Director of Residence Life stating that I was able to get emergency housing through the university. I exhaled a heavy sigh of relief, *I have somewhere to stay. Then guilt hit me in several different directions: But my sisters, my dogs, who will be there for my mother when she needs someone? How could I do this to my stepdad; he'll have to carry this burden by himself? I can't do this, it's not that bad at home; I can keep going.*

Then, my mother texts me: *Hi, where are you and what time are you coming home?* I hesitated and my TRIO-SSS counselor came up to me and said, "Just tell her you're safe, that's all mothers want to know."

I took a deep breath and replied, *I am okay and safe.* To which she replied with threats of calling the police and forcing them to search for me so she can take me back home.

Seriously? How could she not give a crap about how I am or what would cause me to not want to come home? I left her messages unread, not all mothers care about safety.

TODAY'S INSPIRED *Young* LATINA VOLUME III

SCARS

After two days filled with counseling and finding basic living necessities through the many departments and organizations on campus, I was exhausted. However, I barely slept as I fought off nightmares about my sisters screaming for my help, guilt waking me up every few hours. I still attended my classes; I was starving. Well, that part wasn't new. I had spent years restricting my calorie intake, and this day would be no different.

The day of winter formal had finally come, the day that amplified this whole mess. My girlfriend arrived at my room right on time with her pressed suit to get ready together. I sluggishly got dressed. Who has the energy to go to a dance when your life is falling apart? But I already got the dress, so I may as well go. I started curling my hair. As I drifted into thought, I suddenly felt a burning sensation right below my thumb.

"Crap!" I dropped the iron to the table and tried to soothe myself. *Well, that's gonna leave a mark.*

My girlfriend and I made our way to the dance. As we parked, I immediately felt a cold shiver run up my spine, making me nauseous.

"Are you okay?" she said.

I just waved it off and my girlfriend made her way to open the door for me. I stepped out and started walking to the entrance when a car with its high beams on caught both of our eyes as it illuminated us perfectly.

I pulled her to stop walking and squinted towards the car. There they were. My stepdad and my mom staring right back at me. I straightened myself up and grabbed her hand, and walked inside.

"Seriously? What are they doing here?" my girlfriend asked as we found shelter inside. I raised my eyebrows at her and immediately took my phone out to call my TRIO-SSS counselor. She picked up within the first ring and warned us to not leave the premises without an escort to our car and encouraged us to try to enjoy the night.

After a few songs, I couldn't shake the feeling of dread, so I suggested we leave early. First, we had to find someone to walk us out. Luckily, I spotted the Dean of Students Assistant and she was more than happy to walk us out. I searched for my parents expecting high beams to highlight my champagne dress again, but all I could see was an empty parking spot where their car had been earlier. I exhaled a sigh of relief.

A couple weeks passed and I settled into my new arrangement, except that I did not have my identification credentials to apply for a job. My mother had always kept them for me. Requesting replacements of all of them would be a lengthy process, and I needed employment as soon as possible to begin paying off the loans I took out for residence. There was only one solution; I had to go back home.

I knocked on the door assessing the new locks, waiting for someone to open the door. Once I walked into my old home, my sisters greeted me and my dogs jumped for acknowledgement. It felt so welcoming to see those I care for and love. I walked into my room and instantly felt taken back by the energy in the room.

It was unpleasant, but I had things to do. I immediately started stuffing clothes in my limited number of bags. I was going for my identification credentials when I heard my mother walking through the door.

Crap.

I looked up and there she was, staring back at me with a blank expression. I broke the silence with, "Could you give me my identification credentials?"

She looked startled by my voice and motioned for us to talk in private in her room, the same room we last spoke in. Reluctantly I followed with sweaty palms and a racing heart.

"So, what happened Yasmin? Why did you leave? I would like to think that everything was going well. We just had a small disagreement, but I didn't think you would leave. All I said was that you couldn't sleep over that night, but that we could talk about another night," my mother began questioning. I stared at her in disbelief.

"I think it was a little bit more than a small disagreement," I said firmly. "And you definitely did not say that, but if that's how you feel then that's okay. I just came to get my identifying credentials. I don't want to fight with you, but would rather keep it peaceful."

"See, you didn't understand me correctly. That's not what I said that night and if you want more 'freedom' then I'll stop asking you for so many favors. You can take the car to go out with friends and to have fun. You can come back and we will move on as if nothing happened. No one has to know," she pleaded. I nodded processing what I just heard.

"Thank you for considering that, but for now I just want to be away for a while. You should take some time to process what you need to on your own, preferably with counseling and I will do the same. I know you're hurting right now, but I am too. I have been my entire life. You have to start to see things the way they are because I don't want my sisters to reach this point in their lives. They deserve better and you do too," I told her through tears.

My mother had tears streaming down her face as she said, "I'm so sorry. I know you have been through a lot and I have too; from when your father left us and even before that, you know that. But if you come back, everything will be different, okay? I'm sorry." My mother was in the most fragile state I had ever seen her in, sobbing tears of regret and sorrow, to which my maternal instincts replied with embracing her and holding her, telling her it'll be okay.

When we pulled away, she looked for me to say the words she wanted to hear. Instead, I said, "I really hope you do consider going to counseling, not for me but for yourself and for my sisters. They need you. For now, I would appreciate those credentials to keep moving forward."

My mother looked at me in solemn disbelief and left to gather them for me. I immediately put them away safely.

As I walked to the entrance with my family trailing behind me, I said, "Thank you, I should get going. It was nice to see you all."

My Uber driver waved at me, waiting with his trunk open. I loaded my stuff with his help and came back to the doorway to a completely different person. My mother had her usual stern face and disappointed look as I said my farewells to my sisters. When it was her turn, she extended a shorthand which I shook.

Before I closed the door, I said, "Oh by the way, I love the new locks, it's a nice touch." The door shut on my mother's widened eyes.

On the ride back home, I called my girlfriend. She asked for a summary of events and how I was feeling. I replied with my hand on the window with a fresh healing scar under my thumb, "I'm okay." And I meant it.

Every time I look at my scar now, it reminds me that even though it may hurt to choose yourself after a lifetime of consistently serving others, time heals the scars left behind.

THINK YOUNG AND GROW

Growing up in a Hispanic household, children from a young age are taught to never "talk back" out of respect to their parents or elders. This ideology is not new and, while it is rooted in good intentions, it emphasizes to children that their thoughts, concerns and feelings are not as important, or of value. As a result, we grow up not discussing how we truly feel because we believe that it is a negative thing to do or that it is disrespectful. For this reason, I challenge you to make it a habit to express how you feel about something to others who may not realize it. This will reinforce that your feelings are valid and also open to hearing others.

Had I practiced this skill growing up, it would not have been so controversial for my mother to understand my feelings when I finally decided to speak up about not having my own freedom, or how I battled with an eating disorder in her home. I felt that I had no choice but to let two decades of feelings bottle up within me, which I now understand was unhealthy. So, don't be afraid to speak up and let your feelings be known. I assure you that it is worth it.

THIS IS ME

My name is Yasmin Amaro-Garcia. I am a Mexican American, first-generation honors college student currently attending Georgian Court University, pursuing a Bachelor of Science in Nursing. During my lifetime, I hope to encourage Latinx youth to pursue higher education regardless of the circumstances they may be facing, by educating them on the many resources and services available for all.

THE TEN-YEAR PLAN

1. Pursue a Master's in a specialty nursing field and become an educator
2. Publish an autobiography in the hopes of inspiring future generations to persevere amidst adversities and life challenges
3. Establish a sense of clarity and consistency within my family systems

MAKING ROOM FOR TRANSFORMATION

CLAUDIA ROMANI

"The challenge is in making yourself feel uncomfortable so that you can grow."

Ever since I can remember, I have battled with an internal roadblock that has caused me to silence my voice out of fear of being criticized. From a young age, I have internalized the belief that I was simply not good enough; that my voice was not worthy of being heard. Sadly, it is pretty common to hear of people, especially women, say that they do not see their value or worth. I was that girl who did not perceive the goodness that others so adamantly told me I possessed. It was because of my lack of confidence that I denied myself the opportunity to rejoice in my accomplishments and to challenge myself.

TRANSITION

Growing up, I have always had to adapt, to transition. The first instance of transition occurred in September of 2006 when my parents, Armando and Medalith, younger brother,

Gianfranco, and I migrated to the United States from Lima, Peru. After much pondering, my parents left everything behind in search of a better life for their children. We left our first home to start a new one in the land of opportunity. We took our clothes and our steadfast faith with us.

My second home became Paterson, New Jersey; a town that is overflowing with the rich, diverse cultures of the Hispanic, African American, and Bengali communities. Paterson welcomed my family and me as we settled into the second floor of our apartment. With hope in our eyes and the eagerness in our bodies, we were ready to begin a new life full of the opportunities that were not as attainable in our native country as they were in the U.S.

Along with settling into a new country and home came adjusting to a new school. I was a six-year-old student in a class of children with skin of the most beautiful shades of brown. In the beginning, I felt like I belonged because I was in a room with children whom I shared a similar complexion with. However, doubt and fear crawled in every cell of my body when I heard words come out of their mouths. It was the typical kindergarten lingo, but said in English, a completely unfamiliar language to me. I knew not one word of English, and began to feel the pressure and frustration associated with being an immigrant. That was the first time I internalized the false belief that what I had to say was not worthy of being heard because no one could understand me.

Eventually, I learned English, but I could not unlearn the erroneous belief that it was best to remain silent because others would have difficulty understanding me. I rarely spoke up in class, because I was crouched in fear, worried that I would say something wrong. I doubted how well I spoke English. No matter how many English as a Second Language classes I took and how many A's I received in all my classes, I could not find value in my accomplishments.

The doubt I had concerning my English skills stemmed from a bigger insecurity. I was developing this unhealthy habit of comparing myself to others. I used to look at myself as the foreigner who had to try extra hard to fit in, and this mentality was draining. I had settled on the idea that I was just not as good as my peers. I spent all of elementary and middle school depriving myself of expressing all the ideas and dreams I had. My lack of confidence and fear of rejection were growing.

In 2014, I was forced into transition yet again. My parents enrolled me into an eighth-grade program at a private Catholic high school. I was actually eager to start at a new school. This was a great opportunity to meet new people and have a change of scenery. My goals were to excel academically, join the volleyball team, and make new friends.

I did not get the chance to join any sports teams because I chose to focus solely on my classes. However, I did meet my goal of excelling academically and received Principal's List for every quarter that year. I also met my best friend to this day. Everything was going as planned, but that familiar fear of unworthiness crept up that year, and every year of my high school experience.

I was no different than the six-year-old kindergartener who

preferred to keep her mouth shut instead of uttering nonsense. On top of that, I was in a classroom where I was the minority. I had never felt out of place in my previous school because I looked just like everybody else. The feeling of being different added to my perception of my lack of worth. The habit of comparison got worse too, and I felt like I had to try ten times harder to be at the level of my peers. This time I was not only afraid of speaking up because I was not confident in my English skills, but now I felt like a Latina girl did not have much to offer in a room with white students, so I kept my mouth shut again.

THE CONVERSATION THAT CHANGED MY LIFE

It was my senior year of high school, right after a National Honor Society ceremony, when I had a conversation that changed my outlook on life. I was sitting on the bench outside of my high school gymnasium waiting for my ride. Everyone had left after the ceremony; I was the only student left in the building that night.

One of my teachers came up to me and said hello. I responded with a quiet hello and a shy smile. She looked at me a second time and decided to sit next to me. She looked me in the eyes and said, "You're going to college soon. If you do not speak up and stop being shy, no one is going to take you seriously." Ouch.

When I first heard this, I was offended. Does that mean that no one has taken me seriously these past 18 years of my life because I chose to stay quiet? After some reflection, I realized her comment did not come from a bad place. She was trying to warn me. College is a different battlefield and I have to choose whether I want to win or lose my battles. If I did not control my fear of being criticized for saying something wrong or ceased comparing myself to others, then I was never going to become the best version of myself. I had a decision to make that night, and I decided that I was going to change.

Change had been part of my life for as long as I could remember. I had to transition as an immigrant and as a Latina student in a white high school. I did not have a choice in generating those changes. Hearing my teacher say those words pushed me to create change by choice. That was the first time I made the decision to allow transformation to take place.

This moment was such a life-changing experience because it was the first time someone approached me and told me how to improve on something I lacked. I was aware that there were aspects that I needed to improve upon, but I never heard about it from anyone else. I appreciated all the great compliments and positive feedback that I received from teachers and friends because of how I excelled academically, but I never received feedback on how to strengthen my weaknesses. Those weaknesses had never been as visible as they were during that conversation. As I drove home that night, I decided that I was tired of concealing and comparing myself. I had lived all my life afraid of the worst-case scenario, and never gave myself the chance to make an attempt at transforming my fears.

College was my dream and the dream of my parents. I did

not want my fear of speaking up or lack of confidence to prevent me from excelling in college. I needed my voice to advocate for myself and find the opportunities that would ensure my success. I was not willing to give my fears control over my voice anymore.

My teacher was half right that night, because I also recognized that if I wanted to achieve my academic goals, I had to use my voice to network and speak about my skills. However, she was wrong in saying that I would not be taken seriously because of being an introvert. Being an introvert does not mean that others do not admire your work. There is grace in speaking only when you think it is appropriate. Introverts do not always have to say something every five minutes of a conversation, but, when they do, it is because they put thought into their words and believe they add to the conversation. There is nothing wrong with being an introvert. Being different creates a balance in the world.

TRANSFORMATION

I started college with a go-getter mindset. I knew it was the perfect place to turn the page and start building my confidence from scratch. I started building the foundation during the summer of 2018, when I dormed for six weeks at Seton Hall University as part of the Educational Opportunity Program (EOP).

The EOP program provided me with great mentors, advisors, and professors who met me where I was at and worked with me to help me to achieve my goals. The program encouraged me to believe in my abilities and skills. Whenever I doubted myself, my advisor would hype me up and offer techniques to manage my self-doubt and self-criticism. The EOP program taught me to believe in and advocate for myself, which was something I had always struggled to do.

My confidence only grew from there. I spoke up to share my ideas and expressed my opinions. I asked questions and accepted help when I needed it. I took on leadership roles in organizations that I felt passionate about. Currently, I am President of MEDLIFE at Seton Hall University. MEDLIFE is an international nonprofit, which focuses on aiding low-income communities in Latin America and Africa through informational events, fundraisers, and service-learning trips. MEDLIFE's mission is to build an empowering movement to help the poor in their fight for equal access to healthcare, education, and a safe home. This role provides me with the opportunity to be the voice for the vulnerable and marginalized communities of Latin America and Africa. High school me would never have imagined that I would be in a position where I get to be the voice for others.

Growing in confidence involved getting out of my comfort zone. It is easy for me to prefer feeling comfortable because I feel safe, but the challenge is in making yourself feel uncomfortable so that you can grow. One of the most uncomfortable, yet life-changing moves I had to make to build more confidence was accepting to be a speaker at Young LATINATalks, a TedTalks version for Latina women. So many doubts and fears crept up my spine and into my mind as I prepared with the wonderful team for our big day—the day I would conquer my fear of public speaking.

Young LATINATalks permitted me to share my story of how I battled with self-criticism and comparison. I touched upon my struggles with finding confidence in using my voice and ended with advice for anyone in the audience who might have been experiencing similar struggles. The end goal of accepting to speak at Young LATINATalks was to encourage others through my story and provide the tools that helped me to recognize my worth. Before, during and after the talk, I chose to reject all the thoughts in my head that screamed that I was incompetent. Due to my leadership positions and the workshops with the Young LATINATalks public speaking coach, I learned that my voice and story mattered. What I had to share about myself that day was worthy of being heard.

Friends and mentors reached out to me after the event and shared their own experiences with self-criticism and comparison. I felt blessed that they chose to be vulnerable with me and that my talk had such an impact on them. All of them were grateful that I talked about a topic that is so relatable and relevant. Ultimately, I had accomplished my objective of touching others through my story and offering a space to discuss these struggles. By letting go of my fears, I allowed myself to experience one of the most memorable moments of my life. I left that talk with a new sense of confidence and optimism. The impact my talk had on others reassured me that I was going in the right direction.

After making the decision to let my confidence flourish, I realized several truths. My voice matters. My voice helps those in need. My voice has gotten me to the opportunities I have today. My voice is uniquely mine and I will never again be ashamed of using it.

GOD'S BELOVED WORK IN PROGRESS

Over the years, I have grown in confidence and I see myself slowly becoming the person I have always wanted to be. I like to call myself a work in progress. Although, I have reached to levels I never imagined, I am still learning new ways to improve. I still have to remain vigilant of the fears and doubts that roam inside my head, but now I am more aware of how to control them.

Today, I know what I am worth. I am more worthy than what my criticism or, for that matter, what anybody else's criticism has to say about me. I have had to experience such struggles in order to build confidence and find myself. I cannot say that I accomplished all of this by myself. I owe my transformation to God. It is in Him that I found my worth. My faith has reassured me that I am loved and that I am enough to the Father. I am God's beloved work in progress. He works with me at my own pace and never rushes me. He applauds every accomplishment and wipes every tear.

Part of God's plan is the wonderful people He has put into my life. They are people who push me to be better and give me the tools to build my confidence. From the most loving family members to the most supportive mentors, like Somalia and Jes,

God has gifted me the opportunity to cross paths with people who believe in me.

God, my family, friends, mentors, and my dedication have gotten me where I am today. Today, I radiate optimism, confidence, and self-love. I am fearlessly unraveling every gift and talent that God has given me and embracing them. I have what it takes, and so do you. My advice to anyone reading this is to have confidence in who you are and to not be afraid of transition and change because, if you watch carefully, you will witness transition becoming transformation. As St. Catherine of Siena said, "Be who God meant you to be and you will set the world on fire."

THINK YOUNG AND GROW

Even though I have learned from my challenges, I still struggle with maintaining my confidence. Whenever I do cave into doubts and fears, I go back to my favorite acronym that I have created, ARRR. It is an acronym inspired by a podcast I listened to.

Reader, I challenge you to practice these steps whenever you find yourself doubting your abilities.

ARRR stands for Acknowledge, Respira, Release, and Receive.

1. Acknowledge – When I experience a hit on my confidence caused by external or internal factors, I like to start by acknowledging and validating my thoughts without resisting, but not letting them overcome.

2. *Respira* – I choose to *respirar* or breathe in everything that nourishes and is good for me.

3. Release – I release all that contaminates my soul at that moment, and I let go of limitations.

4. Receive – I receive who I am. I accept that I am not perfect, but I tell myself that I am worthy and capable.

Building confidence is a process, but all good things take time. I encourage you to be patient with yourself.

THIS IS ME

I am a Peruvian immigrant and first-generation college student at Seton Hall University in the dual degree program for Psychology and Speech Language Pathology. I dream of becoming a speech language pathologist at a clinical setting, where I can help my future patients build confidence in using their voices to communicate.

In 10 years, I see myself growing spiritually, physically, and mentally.

THE TEN-YEAR PLAN

1. To grow in my faith: I would like to continue to strengthen my relationship with God and improve my prayer life
2. To travel to new countries: I love to travel and immerse myself in rich cultures and languages
3. To learn new languages: My goal is to become fluent in French and Quechua, an indigenous language spoken in my native country, Peru

---

THE INVISIBLE WAR

GABRIELA SURIEL

"I felt there was this stirring in my spirit that did not allow me to rest."

In the silence of my nights, I hear a battle cry similar to the sound of a desperate mother interceding for her child, a cry that shouts from the marrows of my soul. This sounds a bit intense to start off what is supposed to be an inspirational chapter, however, I want to attempt to articulate the seriousness of the silent pain trapped within.

It is like a war impossible to be detected by the human eye. It seems subjective or surreal. Talking about it sometimes is not enough. It is a war that no one understands, not even yourself. This war is the invisible war between two violent forces, flesh and spirit. The terms flesh and spirit may seem a bit spiritual to some, but it is the fight between settling versus thriving in your destiny. It is the fight between good versus great; mediocrity versus excellence; complacency versus fulfillment; temporary pleasures versus everlasting success.

The beauty about this war is that it can be won by choice; the horror of this war is that it can be lost by choice. Choice is a powerful gift God gave us. A gift that I am still unraveling in its complex, yet so simple, nature. Before, I thought that life was merely an event which God lives out through you. I used to believe there was a disparity between decision and destiny, that destiny is what drove our decisions. In essence, there was no choice, because greatness was already predestined for a selected few.

Twenty-five years later, my perspective shifted; I learned that greatness is a choice. Before I share how I arrived at this conclusion, I must provide you with a disclaimer. My story would not mean anything without my belief in Jesus Christ. My life has been a strategic weaving of different threads to create something beautiful. However, my life has not been so smooth. There were unexpected snags and tears throughout the process. People used to console me with the phrase, "God has a plan for you." As if God was going to zap my life to perfection. As I get older, I understand that God's plan is like a moving train, you have to choose to get on it. A wise man once told me, "Good does not always mean God." So which one will you choose, good or God (great)? I am choosing the latter.

MY DEMONS

I took my first breath in the city that never sleeps, New York City, and was raised in the concrete jungle of the Bronx. A clash of hip-hop, merengue, and reggae serenaded the streets. I remember thinking fireworks would go off every now and then. In retrospect, I realize they were gunshots.

The Bronx was home to my most cherished childhood memories. I was blessed to be raised by both of my parents. My mother, Carmen, a former lawyer in the Dominican Republic, traded her dream to follow the love of her life, my father, Luis. Both of my parents immigrated to the U.S.A. because of their faith in "the American dream."

I remember going from daycare to babysitters because my parents would be working long shifts. When asked how I was as a child, my mother would always say that I was *bien tranquila, miedosa y siempre dibujando* (very calm, scared and always drawing). From the outside, it seemed my life was a typical Latino anecdote of a Hispanic family seeking to have a better life. However, there was a reason as to why I was a tranquil and fearful child.

Church bells were ringing, resonating on the brick walls of the buildings in Washington Heights, NY. I remember wearing a white dress that spilled out onto my mother's arms. I was getting baptized in the Catholic Church. Smiles, tears and laughter filled the church's pews. I was being dedicated to God that day and, ironically, I remember I wore the same dress when it first happened.

When I was an infant, I was molested by my cousin who has an undiagnosed developmental disorder. As I was growing up, I would suffer from disturbing nightmares and would experience lucid flashbacks whenever I saw him. I thought it was just a dream until he did it to me again at the age of ten.

As a child, it exposed me to sexuality earlier than I should have been. I did not understand my body and the feelings that I had. At a young age, I was curious about sex, but I felt it was wrong and shameful. Even though I did not comprehend the evil that was done to me, I somehow knew that it was wrong. It's like my spirit knew something that my soul was still trying to understand.

The day it happened, I remembered he wanted to carry me and my mother let him. At the time, I did not know how to walk or speak. I was still a baby. She left the room and he began touching me under my dress. I also remember him using my body to pleasure himself. I remember crying because I felt scared and unsafe. My mother came back into the room and he convinced her to leave me with him. So, she left again. Other explicit things happened that day, which may be too graphic to share, but this event was one of the first memories I had as a child.

I remember having a deep hatred for my cousin. His presence disgusted me. I abhorred the sound of his voice. Hearing him laugh irritated my ears. I saw him every weekend because my parents would visit my grandmother and he happened to live there. My family had compassion for my cousin because he had a developmental disorder, where his brain believed he was younger than he actually was.

I was always looking for opportunities to reveal how evil my cousin was. I remember when I was ten, I barged into my grandma's room to look for something, and I caught him looking at naked women in a magazine. With joy, I ran to my mother because I thought at last he would be exposed. I snitched on him and she grabbed me fiercely and rebuked me. With a firm tone, she said, "Never walk in on him again!"

I thought she rebuked me for speaking up and from that moment, I thought that I was the one who was wrong and that he was right. I decided to hide this skeleton in my closet because my mother's rebuke communicated to me that I would get in trouble for what had happened to me, and so I did not want to tell her because I feared her reaction. I also did not want her to suffer because my mother was a fearful woman who would suffer from anxiety attacks regularly in my early years. Yet, my hate for him continued to fester. It was so pure that I remember feeling satisfied with the thought of him dying.

Molestation was not just an event in my life. It introduced me to other demons that would shackle me. It was an event that opened doors to fears, insecurities, shame, and other forms of darkness. As a result, I have suffered from disturbing nightmares that haunted me until the age of twenty-four. I would often sleep with my parents, even at that age.

I feared the late hours of the night because I felt insecure. I felt like something wanted to take over my soul. My parents did not understand why I was so fearful. I remember my mother asking my aunts to pray for me because I would wake up screaming, or I would cry if I was left alone in my room. My mother would try to trick me into sleeping alone by waiting until I fell asleep and sneakily walking back to her room. This never worked because once I felt the free space on my bed, I would cry until she came back.

By this time, I was already ten, and my parents learned to adapt with me sleeping in their bed. They tried placing a bed next to their bed, but even that did not make me feel safe. In order for me to feel safe, I needed to feel my mother next to me. The nightmares would occur frequently. I would experience sleep paralysis and lucid dreaming. I would see demons in my dreams, and oftentimes I was running. Fear became a permanent resident in my heart and mind. I learned to cater to its whims and live according to its limitations. I developed fear as a form to protect myself. I confused fear with protection.

And fear wasn't the only demon I let in. There were other demons that followed me throughout most of my life. These included shame, deception, trust issues, insecurities, rejection, and self-pity.

SHAME

Molestation taught me the emotion of shame. I was ashamed of my body and felt disgusted with looking at myself naked. I felt ashamed of my femininity. In my childhood, I remember I would dress as a tomboy at times because I felt disgusted with being a girl. I felt uncomfortable dressing "too pretty" because I feared being sexualized. I lived feeling unworthy of love. I felt it was impossible for anyone, especially my own mother, to love me because of what happened to me. I reasoned that as long as I did not share what happened to me, I would be loved. By hiding the truth, I allowed shame to remain.

DECEPTION

This one by far was one of the biggest demons I had to face. Since I kept this secret for so long, unconsciously, I was training my heart and mind to be a skilled deceiver. I was able to hide a monumental secret in my life so well, but I did not know that I was falling deeper and deeper into a pit that I dug myself. Fear is a dangerous thing.

Demons don't often come alone, they bring company. I feared telling the truth because I thought I was protecting myself and my mother. My submission to fear led me to become a skilled liar. I deceived the two people who gave me life. I deceived friends, romantic partners and colleagues. I did not know that I would be creating a detrimental habit that would cost me much pain in my adult life. I chose to deceive others because I was afraid of telling the truth.

TRUST ISSUES

Molestation taught me that no one could take care of me. I learned to take care of myself not out of love, but because of fear. I could not trust my mother to care for me. I could not trust that God could take care of me. I remember that whenever I felt the need to cry, I would take a shower because I did not want my mother to see me cry. I did not like crying in front of people.

In grammar school, when I would get hurt or teased, I would not say anything to my parents. I felt that it was my responsibility to take care of my emotions. I thought my hurt and pains were insignificant. I allowed molestation to become a barrier between my mother and myself, as well as other relationships. I built a wall to protect myself and would push people away if they came close to cracking it down. I became skilled at masking my emotions in front of those that I love.

INSECURITIES

My relationship with insecurities has been a toxic one. There's a distorted form of security that comes from our insecurities. It tricks us into believing what we think is true about ourselves. This can be very dangerous if we do not know ourselves.

I struggled with my identity for as long as I could remember. I never remembered feeling happy with who I was. I always strived to become someone else. I viewed myself as inferior to other people. I would get easily intimidated by other strong women. I always felt like I was lacking something. I never felt complete. I would get anxiety just trying to express what I felt.

It was hard for me to say no to people because I did not want them to dislike me. I was a master people pleaser because I did not want to experience rejection. I looked to polished versions of other women on social media and would tear myself down for not being like them. I felt unattractive and would get jealous of other women because they dressed better or had more drive than I did.

REJECTION

When I told my mother about my cousin looking at nude pictures, her response led me to feel rejected. Rejection can be a very sneaky thing if it is unchecked. I did not know that my shyness would be a result of rejection. I was shy and timid because

I feared being rejected for being true to myself. I people-pleased because I feared rejection. The root of rejection comes from a lack of understanding. My mother's response was not to condemn my pain. She did not know but, because I deceived her, it opened the door to rejection.

SELF-PITY

I lived twenty-four years of my life blaming others and using what happened to me as an excuse to not pursue greatness. Yes, I had the right to be angry with what happened to me and I was entitled to feel the way I did. However, I should not have used what happened to me as an excuse to not go after what God placed in my heart. Molestation taught me the black magic of self-pity. I would wallow in my self-pity and tear myself down whenever something did not happen the way I wanted it to. This affected my relationships with family, romantic partners, friends, and coworkers. Whenever I made a mistake, I would tear myself apart and enslave myself to guilt and shame. I would over apologize for things I did not need to apologize for.

EXPOSURE

All of these demons shared residency in my heart and mind. I learned to normalize my dysfunction and live according to its limitations. Little did they know that their eviction notice was well on its way. The year 2020 was an unexpected dance with unplanned dips and turns. This was the year I lost my rhythm. I lost my ability to flow with the momentum of life's rapids. That year was an introspective interlude as to how I would like to build my life for the next ten years.

Prior to this, I was sleepwalking through life. I graduated college, was blessed with a job, and was in a committed relationship. From the outside, it seemed that I was leading a "normal" life. I had my degree, a salaried job, and a loving partner. Yet, there was a whisper in my spirit that I was suppressing, one that I would often ignore. It was a whisper that evolved into a strident voice: "You are settling with your dysfunction." On the outside, I laughed a lot. I smiled a lot, but in the silence of my nights, I felt empty. I felt compelled to do more research on child sexual abuse. I learned that this is sadly common.

According to the research done by the Darkness to Light nonprofit, one in seven girls and one in twenty-five boys will be sexually abused before their eighteenth birthday. Sixty percent of children are sexually abused by people that the family trusts, which was my case. These statistics may vary because it is estimated that sixty percent of people who are sexually abused will never tell anyone.

Spiritually, I felt discontent. I felt there was this stirring in my spirit that did not allow me to rest. I yearned to lead an authentic life. I wanted to be happy. My soul longed for peace. In January of 2020, I went to a mall so that I could write in my journal. I found a place in a bathroom and locked myself in the room. I sat on the floor and began to journal the pain that had accumulated in my life.

My relationship with my mother was tumultuous because I had lied to her so much about who I was. I had the yearning to be nestled in my mother's arms, but I built a wall with her and expected her to climb it and save me. I wanted to have a fresh start in our relationship, but I did not want to tell her what happened. In the stillness, something beautiful happened. I heard the faint whisper of the Spirit of God say, "You cannot start a relationship with deception; you must tell the truth." This whisper was doused in peace. It was soothing to my soul, and it led me to cry.

God was breaking something in me that day. The wall I had built for years was finally crumbling down. It was a conversation between Him and I. For the first time, I felt safe. I could not believe that I heard His voice. I felt Him encourage me to tell the truth not for my mother, but for me. I understood that in me telling her what happened to me twenty-three years ago, it would help me to tell her of things to come.

God wanted me to rebuild my relationship with my mother. The mother-daughter relationship is an essential relationship because from that bond we learn how to love (Viorst 22). From our mothers we also develop our sense of security (Viorst 22). I chose to push her away, which birthed my insecurities, and feeding the lie that I am unlovable. The deceptive life I led was fueled by hiding my pain. I yearned for a transparent relationship, but that required transparency. I thought my mother would not be able to handle my pain. I thought my vulnerabilities were something to be ashamed of. God reminded me, you cannot heal what is hidden.

That same night, I was faced with a choice. I told my mother as I laid next to her. I cried in her arms and felt the peace of God hover over me. That night I chose to be free. My mother, though speechless at my confession, did not hesitate to embrace me. We both cried together and she looked me in the eye and apologized. She wrapped me in her arms and told me how much she loves me. My journey to healing had just begun.

One of molestation's biggest enemies is exposure. The bible says in Ephesians 5:11-13, to take no part in the unfruitful works of darkness, but instead expose them because any darkness exposed will become light. This verse resonated with my life's story because I was living in darkness. I was communing with my darkness and settling with my dysfunction, instead of exposing it. I was so intimate with darkness to the point that I feared the light. I feared the light because it would expose who I really was. It was difficult for me to believe that the creator of the universe, the one who hung the stars and painted the skies, would see me as worthy. I felt so unworthy of love and God is love (1 John 4:8). That night that I told my mother, I caught a glimpse of God's vast and endless love for me.

STRIPPING AWAY THE HATE

Starting that night, I did not know that I would be embarking on a journey toward inner healing. My confession to my mother made it easy for me to confess to other women in the family. The conversation with my family members allowed me to discover how I was not the only victim. Yet they did not tell anyone of their experience with child abuse because of fear and shame. I also learned that my cousin, the one who I deemed as a monster, was also a victim of child abuse. Strangely, the hate I had for him dissipated. I felt compassion for him and wrote a letter telling him that I forgave him.

Unfortunately, he is not able to comprehend or process emotions well. Therefore, my act of forgiving him was not accompanied with a heartfelt hug and tears of sorrow. I gave him the letter and it was like he did not care. I knew that God was working in my heart because for me to forgive someone who will never have the capacity to apologize for what they did is something I would not be able to do with my own strength.

It takes courage to forgive and to love your enemies. In my choosing to forgive him, I chose to be free; free from the hate that oppressed me and depressed me. I was finally free from the burden of hiding my shame and covering it up. Masking our hurt and pain is a lot of work and takes up a lot of energy. I no longer had to live like that.

Today, at twenty-five, I have chosen to surrender my life to God. There's a lot of skepticism regarding the mystery of surrendering our lives to Christ. I had the false expectation that once I was saved, my life would be filled with rainbows and sunshine. I learned very quickly that this is not true.

There were many unprecedented endings in my life. God was stripping away everything I thought I wanted and who I thought I was. He revealed dreams and visions that were birthed out of fear. He revealed insecurities and jealousies I had over other women. I had finally come face to face with myself. I was once comfortable in the deception that I was leading a "good life." I was comfortable with settling for good and not pursuing great.

My pastor, Steve Hannett of Abundant Grace Church, once said that an eagle that stays in the nest is an eagle that will die and never fly. To fly, you must be willing to fall. I was afraid of getting hurt and was running away from the process of healing. However, I thank God that He stirred my spirit in such a way that I could not rest until I faced what I needed to face. I quit my job and ended my relationship to get closer to God. I felt there was a process I needed to go through before being committed in a relationship. There was a lot of toxicity within me. I understood that in order for me to have a clean slate, I must learn to let go, even if I did not want to let go. I wanted to become who the Lord designed me to become. I have cried many nights and many days. The difference is that I no longer hide my tears. I am not as fearful as I used to be to cry in front of people. Crying in front of people you love does not communicate weakness; in fact, it communicates humanity.

There were days where I felt desperate to run and disappear from the war in my mind. It was and still is a daily battle. My demons were aware of their eviction notice, and their attacks began to get stronger and stronger. It drove me to the point of feeling helpless. I battled depression and would find it hard to get out of bed. Three or four days would go by and I would not even shower.

I had lived to please other people, because I thought that people were my source of love. I thought that people were the ones that approved and validated me, all of which were lies. God is my source of love. He is the one that approves and validates me.

Therefore, I do not need the validation of other people, because I am already accepted.

Knowing and believing must go hand in hand. It's not enough to know that you are loved and accepted. You must believe it. Belief is what drives our actions and our beliefs, usually stemming from our experiences and our thoughts. I kept agreeing with the thoughts that would shout how I am unworthy. In my walk with God, I learned that not all thoughts are mine. I now learn to observe my thoughts and am wary to agree with them. I am not a slave to my mind or my body. I am the one who chooses what I believe. This may seem like an ambiguous path filled with uncertainty, but 2020 taught me to embrace uncertainty. When you finally surrender, there is a freedom that comes with it. The freedom Christ wants us all to have. Surrendering is about living as if you have nothing to defend or hide.

Today I am at peace, something I was unable to experience for twenty-four years of my life. I used to break when the storm would come, but today I bend. Speaking about my trauma has led me on a journey to have hard conversations with my family members. It has allowed me to peel back the superficial layers that can exist and delve deep into the pain that's often hidden before our very own eyes.

God has rebirthed my passion for community development and serving impoverished neighborhoods. This passion has led me to enroll in a Bible college that focuses on missionary work. I hope to serve in Costa Rica for three months and enroll in a master's program that focuses on the development of a community. My goal is to one day have a nonprofit of my own that serves underserved youth through faith, the arts, affordable housing and healthy living.

Although my life seems to be swimming in the eddies of uncertainty and unprecedented endings, the beauty is that every ending precedes a beginning. It is all a matter of choice. I chose to leave what was familiar to delve into the unfamiliar. I chose to leave the shore and dive into the depths of my calling. I can finally say without reluctance, that I am enjoying who I am becoming. Deception no longer rules my life. My shame and fear are still a work in progress, but I am not where I used to be, and I thank Jesus for that.

Sources:

Viorst, Judith. "Necessary Losses". New York, NY, Fireside, 1998.

THINK YOUNG AND GROW

Journaling has been an essential tool to my emotional and mental wellness. Take some time to reflect where you are in your life. What do you need to heal from and where do you want to go? Answer intentionally and may your pen be driven by your heart.

Finally, create a vision book that captures your heart's desires. Be as creative as you want. You can draw pictures or insert magazine images of things that you want in any area of your life. Each page should reflect an aspect of your life (physical, family, love, career, spiritual, mental health, etc.). Once you are done, keep it in plain sight, and when the year ends, review what you've accomplished.

Prayer

Prayer is a conversation with God. You can be honest with God. He knows our hurt and our pain better than anyone. We are meant to lead a life of abundance if we choose Him. To choose Him means to choose the very one that gives life and not death. Lead a life submitting to love and surrendering what burdens us. We all suffer and we all experience pain, but your joy will come if you believe. I wrote down a prayer as an example:

Father, thank you for your mercies and your goodness. I pray that you lead me and guide me to fulfill everything you have written for me to do. Help me be aligned with your plan. Reveal the thing I must let go of and give me the courage to pursue what I must. For you have not given me a spirit of fear but of power and of love, and of a sound mind (2 Timothy 1:7). I ask this in Jesus's mighty name, Amen.

THIS IS ME

My name is Gabriela Maria Suriel and I am the proud daughter of Luis and Carmen Suriel, who traded their dream just so that I can have one of my own. I have an affinity for the arts and serving the community, which propelled me to earn a Bachelor's in Psychology and minor in Fashion Design from Montclair State University.

Since then, I have been involved in many altruistic projects. From tutoring students in prison to teaching Latina mothers how to sew to leading a ten-mural project in the community of Paterson, NJ. All that I seek in life is to learn how to serve with humility and lead an authentic life rooted in Christ.

THE TEN-YEAR PLAN

1. Start a nonprofit school that merges faith and the arts, and includes a curriculum that focuses on empathy and emotional healing for children

2. Graduate with a Master's of Arts in International Community Development with a focus in Education

3. Have a family of my own

BETTER DAYS

TATIANA HART

"I was put here to impact and to give back."

I was broke and broken. I went from living a worry-free life to sitting in my room everyday with nothing but my darkest thoughts and fears. Everything that I valued and thought I needed in my life was gone. I was left with the two things I didn't value enough at the time, but later realized were the only two things I've ever needed: Trust in myself and in God.

For five months, I was forced to have a drastic reality check with myself. I was at a point where it was a true matter of life or death. I was at war with myself, and eventually threw in the white flag to suicidal thoughts, constant panic attacks, meltdowns, and so much more. Dealing with mental health issues is similar to dealing with a broken bone. When you break a bone, in many cases you will have to seek medical care. From there you may have to wear a cast, take pain medicine, and get physical therapy, etc. The same goes for mental health issues; you may have to seek medical care, you may have to take medication, and you may have to go through the long-term work with a professional to heal.

THE BEGINNING SIGNS

Since I was a child, I've always struggled with anxiety. I was raised in a military family, and my norm was always moving to a new state and school. I never allowed myself to get comfortable in places because I knew I would not be there for long. From Kindergarten to twelfth grade I attended seven different school districts in four different states. My experience was unique because military children relocate and readjust more often than average students. Most schools are not familiar with our lifestyle and needs, and this impacts our social and emotional growth. This is important, because these are our formative years. Having very little support and understanding from school leaders and my peers affected my relationship building skills.

My sophomore year of high school I moved from California back to southern Illinois. I was attending a predominantly white high school, one of six African American/Latina students, surrounded by views of cornfields and farms. At this school it was hard trying to fit in while experiencing racism firsthand. During my time at this high school, I witnessed what it felt like to have racist jokes and comments made to me.

I remember having my first full-blown panic attack my sophomore year of high school. It felt like I was stuck in a very small and dark room; the air was so thin, it felt like I couldn't breathe. My body was flooded with fear to the point that I couldn't even move. The darkness began to consume me, and I felt like I was going to die. However, this was not my first episode dealing with anxiety.

There is a condition called Separation Anxiety Disorder (SAD), where children experience excessive distress when they have to be away from their source of comfort, usually a parent or caregiver. If you were to ask my mother, she would say I have suffered from this disorder since the day I was dropped off at daycare. When we would get in the car, I would begin to cry because I knew I was getting dropped off. I would cry for the first hour or two after being dropped off, and eventually be okay the rest of the day.

As far back as I can remember, in elementary school, I still suffered from separation anxiety. I remember my first day at my new school in third grade, my parents were dropping me off and I cried the entire ride there. My mom dropped me off at my classroom and left. I remember, running out of the classroom and heading towards the door. My mom stopped me and I had a full-blown meltdown. This lasted almost every day from Kindergarten through most of fourth grade.

By seventh grade, my separation anxiety went away, but a new form of anxiety creeped in. I was starting a new middle school in California. I felt I was an oddly shaped child; I was tall and extremely skinny, and due to my poor posture, my mother insisted on buying me a rolling backpack. I was so embarrassed by this and the new kids must have smelled it on me because they bullied me and constantly made fun of me. This public humiliation impacted how I viewed myself, trying to fit in at middle school, and how I developed relationships/friendships.

By the time I got to high school, I started accepting people in my life who were toxic, but I didn't realize it at the time. For example, one of the friendships I tried to nurture was with a male friend my sophomore year of high school. We connected because we were two of the few minority students at that school. One day, we were hanging out in the neighborhood and he grabbed me aggressively and I slapped him across the face. I immediately called my mom because I did not know how to process the situation, which resulted in me having another panic attack. Needless to say, my relationship with that young man didn't last long because my family and I moved at the end of that school year.

Junior year we moved to northern Illinois, where I began at a new high school which was predominantly a minority school. This was my third high school in two years! Now that I was getting older, I had a different sense of self, I felt more developed in my diverse experiences, and a little more confident about my appearance. I switched from rolling backpacks to purses and my body was taking its feminine form.

With my newly developed confidence, this attracted a newer form of bullying. This time around, the bullying was a little more aggressive and almost resulted in physical altercations. I made one friend, but this was not enough to shelter me from the verbal assaults, which came daily. I had a couple of additional relationships that were extremely toxic and abusive. All of these experiences were contributing to a breaking point that no one, not even myself, was prepared to cope with.

In 2018, I graduated high school. I was given more freedoms and privileges by my parents. I was able to stay out later and drive my friends around. With this new found freedom, I began making poor choices in friends and relationships. As a result of my toxic relationships in high school, I became disconnected from my emotions, my family, and my own self-control. I was fighting with my parents daily and began running away. What I realize today is that I was spiraling out of control because all of the demons that had plagued me were now controlling my poor judgement.

One summer day, I got to my lowest point and attempted suicide. I remember waking up that day extremely angry at the world and even the smallest things would upset me. That afternoon, my mother and I got into a heated argument, which resulted in me trying to take my own life. This small argument was my breaking point, and I was finally waving the white flag. I could no longer bear the constant pain of anxiety, anger, confusion, and sadness every day. That evening, I was admitted into a treatment center for care, and I was forced to remain there for three days.

I'll never forget one visit with my sister, we were not as close then as we are today, but as she left our visit, she hugged me hard and began to cry because she was worried about me. That was the moment that helped me realize I was so loved by my family, and I needed to have more love for myself. When I returned home from the treatment center, I accepted this as a fresh start.

THE TEST

In the summer of 2018, I began a new job working in a management role at a family-owned business, I had my own car, and I felt financially independent. I've always been the type of person to look for opportunities where I can develop and grow to take the next steps in life. Now that I have graduated, I began feeling the pressure of figuring out what I wanted to pursue as a career. As a result of this, I was ready to leave my management role and seek my next step.

As a believer in God, whenever I am confused, worried, or need guidance, I always seek Him. My family raised me to love and obey God. One of my favorite Bible verses is Matthew 6:33, "But seek first his kingdom and his righteousness, and all these things will be given to you as well." So that's exactly what I did, when I knew I was no longer meant to be at my job, I prayed out to Him and asked Him to show me what it was he wanted me to do, and to show me where he needed me to go.

At first, I thought the answer God was going to give me was going to be a simple one and an easy transition, but God had other things in mind for me. Usually when I needed guidance and pray to God, the answers from Him were always vivid and clear. The same day I prayed to Him, and asked Him to show me what I needed to do, I got into a car accident that almost killed me and the other driver. I completely totaled my car and, ironically, I ended up having to quit my job since I no longer had transportation.

I was so upset and confused by this universal response, that

I was paralyzed with fear: fear from driving, fear from going out, and a fear from praying. This accident reactivated my anxiety. I was afraid of driving because of how horrific the accident damage was to both cars. It truly was a miracle that I survived. I was afraid to pray because usually when I asked God for guidance, it has always been smooth and easy, whereas, this time it was loud and hard.

I didn't understand why God would take everything I thought I needed away from me. I felt that if I were to pray, something bad would happen to me again. For five months, I stayed home with no one to talk to—I had no friends, no relationships, just myself, my family, and God. I was forced to spend my time in self-reflection where I struggled to answer questions like: *Who am I? What type of person do I want to be? Do I love the person I am today?*

One thing that hit me during my reflection was what I had feared most: not having purpose. I believed that having a job and a car gave me a sense of purpose and some sense of financial independence. I had invested so much time and energy into material things, and trying to make others happy by buying their validation. In the end, I received nothing in return. I was so focused on success and quick wins, that I was not paying attention to what would ultimately need my attention the most: my physical, spiritual and mental health.

During my healing process, I had to remind myself and be reminded by my family that I was still very young. Being only seventeen, I did not know enough about the adult world because

I had been taken care of most of my life. My family helped me apply the everyday homework my therapist was assigning to me, such as showing more gratitude, taking time for myself, etc.

INVEST IN YOURSELF

My healing process is a journey, and some days are easier than others. I remember taking a look in the mirror one evening, after being locked away in my room, and feeling so mentally exhausted and wanting to feel strong again. Remember what I stated at the beginning of my story? "Dealing with mental health issues is similar to dealing with a broken bone." I no longer wanted to feel suffocated in my dark emotions and was ready to go through the necessary steps to heal my mental health.

The first step I had to take to begin my journey of healing was to practice forgiveness. I wanted to forgive those who hurt me in my past, but it required me to first forgive the one holding on to all of the baggage: myself. I was so mad at myself for not controlling my anxiety, accepting toxic and abusive relationships, and for trying to take my own life. I realized I was not healing properly, and I knew this was not a task I could do myself.

I made a brave and vulnerable decision to see a cognitive behavioral therapist. I shared my struggles with anxiety and that I wanted to move forward in my healing, but forgiveness was difficult. She suggested I write letters and the first series of letters go to the individuals I was having a hard time forgiving, including my old friends, my bullies, my exes, and lastly myself. My therapist also introduced me to meditation. With prayer and meditation, I began to heal and finally forgive myself for not knowing any better about the choices I made around toxic relationships and self-harm.

During my meditation sessions, I began receiving visions, or as my mentor would say having a "divine download." In my meditation sessions I would go into a deep, meditative state. This meditative state would completely relax my mind, body, and soul. Think of it as being in a calm, tranquil room with complete silence, and all you can hear is your thoughts. These were the moments when I had no feelings of anxiety, stress, worry, etc. I was able to visualize and dream of myself speaking in front of crowds, traveling the world and writing a book. I believe these visions showed me the direction I needed to go towards to heal and grow. I began to discover my purpose.

One weekend my mother and I turned a wall in my room into a blank chalkboard canvas. It was a symbol for me to continue to push forward and see my goals. I printed out pictures of my dream car, a passport, and a check that would pay off my parents' mortgage. I had key Bible verses and sticky notes with words of affirmation written on the wall. Seeing this "vision board" renewed my faith in a greater plan for my life.

A few months after my car accident, I got a call from a friend asking me if I would like to learn about an investment opportunity about the foreign exchange market. At first I was hesitant. I was completely broke and I had no money or job. After praying to God about the opportunity, my hesitation soon turned into excitement. I discovered this opportunity was a chance for me to grow in my healing process. I decided to take a chance. Today I am so grateful, because what I didn't know was that this experience would open so many new doors and reveal to me a journey towards my purpose in finance.

As I continued to grow personally and financially from this investment opportunity, I began to look forward to trying new things. I chose to travel on my own for the first time and was open to experiencing new environments. I had the opportunity to travel to Houston, Atlanta, and Costa Rica, and meet new people from all over the world. Even during these times, I was still dealing with my anxiety. While meeting new people I was extremely cautious on who I created relationships with. I made sure to set boundaries with myself and others, and I continued to practice meditation and gratitude.

As I was creating a balance in my life, I became more interested in learning about the subject of finance. I enrolled in college for a degree in business and attended professional events with topics around finance. I am currently pursuing a certification as an enrolled agent, which led to a new job as a tax specialist.

During my education, I had a realization that I was never taught about the basics of finance in school or at home. I did not know how to open a bank account in my own name, file a tax return, get a loan to purchase a car, establish credit or understand student loan debt. As a result of this realization, I created my own business. Green T Wealth Inc., a female, minority-owned business which offers financial services that will ultimately become a resource to empower and educate generations to come.

As I reflect back on my journey through anxiety and depression, receiving therapy and discovering a passion in financial empowerment, I now know my purpose. I was put here to impact and to give back. Although it's been quite the journey that's still far from over, I now know I was put here to impact individuals about the importance of finance, and give back through philanthropic donations to the minority community. My purpose is clear and my heart, my faith, and my mind are now aligned.

THINK YOUNG AND GROW

To anyone who is currently battling mental health issues, I encourage you to keep going. Keep fighting the war, don't wave the white flag, and seek help. One thing I wish I knew then that I know now, is that everything is going to be okay!

One of the best pieces of advice I was ever told was, "You become what you think about." It takes practice, but being cognizant about your thoughts makes a huge difference in your mental health. Focusing more on the positive things can help flush out the negative thoughts. I suggest you keep yourself busy, whether it's finding a new hobby, working out, meditating, or creating a vision board looking forward to accomplishing future goals.

Lastly, to those who are struggling to forgive, I suggest you write a letter. Whether it's to yourself or to someone else. Forgiving plays a huge role in every healing process. Just know that you are not alone.

Suicide Hotline: 800-273-8255

THIS IS ME

I am Tatiana Hart, a creative, independent and entrepreneurial-minded Afro-Latina. I am committed to empowering minorities, millennials and GenZ to create generational wealth and discover their true purpose.

As founder of Green T Wealth Inc., my initiatives include developing professional networks in financial literacy, women in finance, and trading experts within the financial industry.

THE TEN-YEAR PLAN

1. Become an international keynote speaker

2. Become a philanthropist

3. Obtain my Master's degree in FinTech (Financial Technologies)

BECAUSE YOU CAN

MARLENE MEDINA

"I was an immigrant unwanted in this place that I called home."

MY ROOTS

I cannot begin telling you about me without first telling you about my family. My parents are my backbone. My dad is the smartest person I know. Born and raised in Guanajuato, Mexico in 1974 to a humble family, at a young age he had to start working to help to provide for his family. For this reason, he only got to finish elementary school, but my dad has never stopped learning. My dad's brain works in mysterious ways. While he might not have received a formal education, he can fix just about anything from a phone to a washer to a car. He claims they all "work" the same, just in different scales. No challenge is too big for my dad. This is where I get my "anything is possible" attitude.

My mom was also born and raised in a small town called Panama, Mexico. She is from "el rancho," where school was not really a main priority, especially for a girl. She endured pain at a young age having lost her mom at the age of five to cancer. I think that is what makes her love a little harder and feel a little more. My mom is my best friend. She is quick to make friends, from the person she is waiting in line with to the cashier checking her out. My mom's laugh is the most heartwarming sound. From my mom, I learned to be nice and kind to every person I cross paths with.

My mom and dad met at young age and became pregnant at the ages of sixteen and eighteen. They were just kids, but they knew they wanted a better life for my sister and me. I feel blessed to say I had an overall very happy childhood. I was born in Guanajuato, Mexico in 1995. Every morning, I would wake up to my dad carrying me to our kitchen where my mom and my older sister were making breakfast. I would spend all day from sunrise to sunset outside with my sister, Alejandra, and our dog, Guerro. We grew up surrounded by aunts, uncles, and cousins.

From what I can remember, everything was pretty perfect. What I did not know, was that my dad would spend months in the United States working crappy jobs to make enough money to come back to us and pay for our expenses. My mom was not a fan of spending time away from my dad, so she packed her bags and headed to the United States. My mom left me at five and my older sister at six with our grandparents for a few months, while she and my dad made enough money to have my sister and I join them.

Eventually, my parents sent for us and we arrived in our new home in Joliet, IL. It was snowing that day, and the cold was unlike anything I had ever experienced, but none of that mattered. My mom was waiting for us, along with our new baby sister.

Growing up, I was not aware of my undocumented status. It was not until I entered high school that it finally mattered. I was sixteen and ready to get my driver's license when, to my surprise, I could not. At that moment nothing made sense. I was an immigrant unwanted in this place that I called home. I not only could not get a driver's license; I also could not get a job or apply for FASFA. How was I supposed to start my life in a place that I called home, yet it rejected me in every way possible? I did not want anyone any one to know of my situation. To sixteen-year-old Marlene, being an immigrant meant shame. I did my best to hide it from my peers. I oppressed my own culture fearing that my peers would know I was immigrant if I acted "too Mexican."

DECISIONS

In August 2012, a few months before my seventeenth birthday, my life and those of 826,000 young adults changed! Deferred Action of Childhood Arrivals, better known as DACA, was introduced. I remember my parents rushing my older sister and I to see our lawyer. While I did not fully understand what was going on, I knew it was a moment of celebration. I could feel my mom's excitement. From this moment, my life changed. I had this unexplainable fire ignite within me. I was given an opportunity, and I was not going to let it go to waste. I immediately got my driver's license, started my credit, and got a job.

I graduated high school in 2014, and was conflicted about what was next for me. I always knew I wanted to go to college, yet at home there was never much talk about it. My parents always encouraged education and good grades, but to them and me, college still seemed like a far-fetched dream. One day I came home late after work and my dad was up. He knew I was at a crossroads, lost and not really knowing what was next for me.

He looked at me and told me with hesitation, "If you want to go to college, you will have to make it happen on your own. I do not have the money to support you." I think I knew it all along, but hearing it out loud was hard.

Now what? I thought. I was meant for more than just being a cashier at McDonalds. That is when I decided to save all my checks to enroll in a nearby community college, Joliet Junior College. I enrolled the week before school started, not knowing what I was getting myself into, or if I would finish.

A month or so into school, things seemed to be working out. I was going to school full-time and working part-time as a teller at TCF Bank. Eventually, tuition and my expenses were starting to add up and after a year at community college, I had to start working full-time while going to school part-time. I really did not have anyone to guide me, as I was going through this change in my life. My parents did not understand what college was like, my closest friends had gone away to college, and I was too scared to reach out to my school for guidance. But somehow, I managed to come up with a plan, and was more certain about what I wanted and how I could achieve those goals. I was going to graduate JJC and attend a four-year university, where I would get my degree in accounting. I would buy a car and become a supervisor at TCF. I was focused and determined.

I graduated JJC, I got my first car, and became the new supervisor a TCF Bank at the age of twenty. I started the process to transfer to the University of Saint Francis. That is when I came to a halt, my counselor told me that I was missing some credits and would probably need to do an extra semester at Saint Francis. I had money saved up for two semesters and would work to get the money for my third and fourth semester. As a DACA recipient, I could not apply for financial aid or a student loan. I could not afford an extra semester.

I asked my counselor for options. She said I could return to JJC and finish those credits there. While that was not what I wanted, it was the best and cheapest option.

Meanwhile at work, an opportunity presented itself. A position for assistant manager opened, and I was interested. However, the position was in Glendale Heights about 45 minutes from Joliet. I was about to be enrolled in a four-year university as a full-time student, but if I took this job, then that would mean that I made it, right?

I told my parents my plan. I would take this job and drop out of school because this is what I had been working for. My excitement as a twenty-two-year-old over this opportunity clouded my judgement. My dad looked at me, "Marlene, you think this is a good opportunity, but this is one of many you will have after you graduate. School should be your main priority."

I looked at him and said, "But, Dad, I will be making good money. I will be able to help you more. I won't have to pay for school." I thought about what my Dad had said, and he was right. I needed to finish school. It is easy to get caught up in the excitement of the moment and forget what the end game is. I am thankful I had the support and guidance of my parents to continue school.

The next day I called the manager to withdraw my application and explained that school was my main priority at the moment. He understood and that was that, or so I thought. He called me later that night and asked me to reconsider. He explained that he had gone to school and worked full-time as manager. He told me that it was possible to do both and that he was willing to work with my schedule. I told him I needed to think about it.

I was not sure how was I supposed to go to school full-time and work full-time traveling 45 minutes to work each day. I told myself I just needed to be organized and plan. So, I took the position. For two years, I had no days off. I would be at school Mondays, Wednesdays, and Fridays and work Tuesdays, Thursdays, Saturdays, and Sundays.

At moments, it seemed impossible. I worked hard even when I did not feel like it; I took every moment as an experience; I tried to be the best Assistant Manager and student I could be. I gave my all day in and day out. Then the day I was waiting for came: Graduation day. It was everything I had imagined and more. All those sleepless nights and early mornings were so worth it. Seeing my mom and dad as I walked the stage is a moment I will never forget.

My parents might not have been able to provide me with a

college fund, but they supported me in so many more ways. My mom would bring me a plate of fruit as I stayed up finishing homework. My dad would change my car's oil as I caught up on sleep on a Sunday afternoon. My immigrant parents gave me strength. I was ashamed that my friends would judge me if they knew my parents were immigrants, if they knew I was an immigrant. But that was not the case anymore. I became proud of my roots, proud of my parents. They are my hidden source of power. I know strength, courage, and determination because of them. Everything that I was accomplishing was because of them.

Between all the chaos of life, between being a daughter, a sister, a student, and working woman, I realized that everything I needed I already had within me.

LIFE AFTER COLLEGE

A few months after graduating college, I landed my first accounting job as a staff accountant. This job really pushed me out of my comfort zone and challenged me in many ways. I had previous experience as an accountant, but as we all know, school is a lot different from the real world. I went to school for accounting but working there was not at all how I had pictured. There was not a lot of support or training, which made me feel discouraged and like I was not "smart" enough for this job.

I held on and slowly started to make sense of things. I spoke up and asked for help and did research on my own to learn more about what I was doing. It has been a year since I started that job, and I am now ten times more comfortable.

My goal has never been to just be an employee, to put in my eight hours, and call it a day. I decided to start a career in accounting because I wanted people, like my parents, to have someone they could communicate with when it came to their finances. I want to be a resource to my community, to provide trust and expertise. This mindset has led me to start my journey of becoming a CPA.

Do I feel prepared or ready? No, but in life you often must start before you are. I recently signed up for the study material and after logging in for the first time, I panicked. There is so much material to go over. The feeling of doubt started to creep in. *Who do I think I am thinking I can pass this exam?* I allow myself to feel scared and anxious for a few minutes, then jump into my plan of attack.

First, addressing those negative thoughts, why do I feel like I cannot pass it? What is overwhelming? Then, creating a schedule and, finally, putting it out into the universe. "I will put in the time and effort required to make this work. I will have fun while studying. I will put my heart into this experience, and I will come out a CPA." I have already knocked down many walls set for an immigrant Latina woman, why should this be any different?

THINK YOUNG AND GROW

As a woman, a minority and an immigrant, I have been told "no" time and time again. I have been told that I could not go to college. I have been told "no" to pursuing my career. I have been told I do not belong. If I had listened to even just one of those no's, I would not be the person I am today. I challenge you to push back on those no's. I challenge you to push back on those feelings of insecurity and fear that often stop us from reaching further.

THIS IS ME

My name is Marlene Medina and I am a Mexican immigrant from Guanajuato, Mexico. I am the daughter of Jorge and Maribel Medina. I am a sister to my five amazing siblings: Alejandra, Alisia, Jorge, Abigail, and Lucy. I am a recent graduate from University of Saint Francis. I am an accountant, and have recently decided to advance my career and started my journey to become a CPA.

I love to cook and volunteer as a Girl Scout troop leader. For a long while, I felt that being a DACA recipient was a huge disadvantage, but decided to use it as a driving force instead. I aspire to be a role model for all young girls and future generations.

THE TEN-YEAR PLAN

1. To become a Certified Public Accountant (CPA)
2. To visit my hometown, Guanajuato, Mexico
3. Learn to cook without following a recipe

GROW, GLOW, AND THRIVE

MICHELLE RAMIREZ

"Acknowledging the importance of mental health has been crucial in learning to face adversity and fulfillment."

My name is Michelle Ramirez and I was born in Los Angeles, California. At the age of three, my family moved to Chicago and since the age of ten, we have lived in Cicero, IL. The communities we have resided in are predominately Latinx and Spanish-speaking. My mother is from San Salvador and my father from Oaxaca, Mexico. I am the second oldest sister and come from a family of six. Being first generation Latinx, I have learned to overcome personal and professional challenges. Throughout my journey as a young Latina, I have come to appreciate the challenges faced as they have impacted and shaped who I now am.

Growing up, my family had basic essentials and little room for leisure expenses. Overall, we grew up being low income. Once, my *mami* fed us, four children, with two eggs and tortillas. Though my parents did their best to cover the financial difficulty, our financial status became very evident when I was transitioning into my first year of college at DePaul University. This was the year my father had been injured at work and only worked a couple of months. When FAFSA time came around and I saw the income tax documents, the income ranged around $15,000.

Back then, I knew we had a tight socioeconomic status, but it is only years later that I realize how incredibly low that income was for a family of six. Once I received my award letter from school and saw the many zeros in granted scholarships and loans, I made a very important promise to myself on that day, a promise that I still live by and hold dear to my heart. Looking at that letter, I promised myself that I would not let our income status limit my future. I decided that one way or another, my future would consist of exciting experiences, happiness and successes.

ECONOMIC BACKGROUND

Through my four years in college, I had many times when I felt like taking a leave from school to focus on work would be best. I would visit the office of financial aid numerous times hoping for new finance opportunities. Unfortunately, loans were my only option. In fact, a financial aid advisor even suggested I take time off instead of guiding me to financial aid appeals, internal or external scholarships, knowing the likelihood of returning to school upon taking a leave would be less likely. This advice was not very encouraging at all. Luckily, my parents were very supportive. Even though they did not fully understand the U.S. education system, they made sure we had the best foundation possible to continue our studies.

As the years went on and exposure to resources continued, I was able to connect with other women of color mentors who understood my Latinx low-income background, and the importance of not taking a break from school to finish my degree. Women who, instead of guiding me to leave school, encouraged me to find scholarships from local restaurants to higher, nonprofit based ones, or helped me brainstorm different personnel to speak to and explore other possibilities such as double counting a course to fulfill two credits instead of one. These influential women led me to many "aha" moments. The moments of realizing that if you really set your mind to it, you can overcome the hurdles laid in front of you. They were my constant reminder that I indeed belonged at the university, despite some staff and students who made it feel like low-income, brown women didn't belong.

One mentor in particular encouraged me to apply for a $3,000 scholarship. Initially, there was no way I could imagine being awarded that. Maybe this thought came from internalized doubt and fear of failure. Deep in my heart I longed for this scholarship in so many ways. I wanted to not worry about finances and enjoy the learning process. I wanted to secure my enrollment in the quarter in order to be fully present in class and partake in enriching conversations. I firmly believe that because of the purity of that energy and hope to be awarded the scholarship, as well as my academic record and dedication, I was awarded the scholarship. Inevitably, I realized the power of empowerment amongst a community of dedicated women in order to build creative and determined leaders.

Likewise, growing up low income meant having limited exposure to the world. I had never traveled outside the state, much less the country. During the first year of college, I saw numerous opportunities to study abroad. I would visit the study abroad office and put into the universe that I too wanted this experience that many other students had. At that point, I did not even have a passport.

One day I came across a ten-day trip to Athens, Greece for first year students that caught my eye. I applied for the class, a scholarship and for my passport! To my surprise, I was accepted to enroll in the class and also received financial aid for a portion of the trip. Traveling to Europe was something I never thought I would do. From boarding the huge plane to being with my classmates in an unknown country, it was an unbelievable experience to visit the places we read about in class.

From the first year of college until the end of my undergraduate experience, every day was a reminder of the endless opportunities offered to low-income students. Even though it came with taking on more jobs and student loans, these incredible experiences reinforced that I deserved to be in a private institution, just as much as others that potentially had parents that donated buildings and came from wealthier financial backgrounds. Four years later, I crossed the stage and earned my bachelor's degree from the private, prestigious institution of DePaul University. I proudly and boldly decorated my graduation cap to read Chingona and wore my half Mexican and half Salvadoran sash as I received my degree.

Realizing you can and are deserving of greatness sets you in the path to receiving an abundance of opportunities. After realizing I could travel, I began to plan trips to Mexico to meet my paternal family. Shortly after, I traveled to El Salvador with my mom to visit and meet her family. These trips have been meaningful in developing a deeper understanding of my culture, background and our own stories. I have learned to acknowledge my history, those that came before me, and to understand how I have come to be.

CULTURAL NORMS

Regardless of the admiration and appreciation for my background, I am also critical of how detrimental practices deriving from toxic masculinity can be. Generally, our culture has traditional expectations for women that limit our success. Women are taught to cater to the needs of others—of partners, children and family—and to have little regard for our own wants and needs. Our culture tends to teach women to self-sacrifice their happiness, peace, and wellbeing for that of their family. Realizing that my life did not have to consist of those characteristics has guided me to explore more liberating ways of life. In doing so, I have realized the most essential decision we have is the power to choose what parts of our culture we want to filter out and which we want to continue implementing. We have the ability to let go of toxic masculinity practices and embrace a more self-fulfilling way of life. This means breaking generational cycles, unlearning toxic cycles, and relearning how to love ourselves into a joyful life. These are changes that have not come easy, but that are life changing in ways I would otherwise not have imagined.

In my early twenties, I was living with a partner. It was only towards the end of our relationship that I realized he was actually mentally, emotionally, and financially abusive. He would say mean things to me and would often make me feel worthless. He would repeat negative comments over and over, to the point that I inevitably started to internalize them. I felt that what he said was right and that I was in fact, out of my mind. It took him punching a hole in the wall for me to be scared and really wonder if my face or body was next.

Thankfully, my *mami* has taught me what it means to be a *mujer hecha y derecha.* She has taught me that this was not a way of living a happy life. I moved out, went to domestic violence therapy, and began my path to healing. For a couple of months, I was on medication for anxiety and to help with my sleeping patterns. Reaching out to these resources was not easy. It was scary and different because I was not used to hearing about women going to therapy, leaving their spouses for mal-treatment, or seeing a psychiatrist for mental support. As I made these changes to my life, I grew prouder by the day of the steps I had taken to live a better life. The more I shared my journey with those around me, the easier these conversations became.

I grew up learning that *"la ropa sucia, se lava en la casa"* (dirty clothes get washed at home.) It is important to note that growing up, I did not really have anxiety or panic attacks. My parents were always great at ensuring we were peaceful and felt safe. At first,

MICHELLE RAMIREZ

I wanted to hide the experience, but that did not serve me well. Instead, I embraced my experience and used it to move forward. Speaking and sharing in detail of how I did not know how to cope with anxiety or the ways anxiety/panic attacks manifest themselves in self-hurting, such as hair pulling or scratching my skin, has never been a cheerful experience for me to share. This has mostly been because these topics are still relatively radical for some in our community.

In the early stages of my healing process, I would start speaking about it and would cry as I shared with my therapist and friends the effects caused by the abuse. However, having the same conversation with my immediate family has always been more difficult given their own comfort level with these topics. Now, a couple of years after, though still in an ever-growing healing journey, I am able to speak and analyze why I, like many other women, stayed in that space. Though I don't applaud myself for dealing with much of that toxic relationship, I do applaud myself for knowing when to step away, put my well-being first, learning to be healthier and for immersing myself in spaces that help me thrive. Had I not had the experience I did, I probably would not be the fierce, unapologetic, *chingona* and *chillona* I am now.

VAMOS CON TODO

Of course, when facing difficult times, it is not easy to look toward the bright and shining light. When I was undergoing the challenges of obtaining my educational career and unhealthy relationship, my shoulders often felt heavy. My neck was tight;

I was navigating through the challenges. Fortunately, I learned to acknowledge that I did not have adequate or effective coping mechanisms and accept my need to seek ways of caring for myself, physically and mentally. This was how I encountered one of the most valuable characteristics of my life: having a healthy mind. Acknowledging the importance of mental health has been crucial in learning to face adversity and fulfillment. It has taught me to face challenges with grace and embrace them in ways that are empowering and a motivation to reaching the tasks I hope to achieve. Rather than letting challenges take over, I attribute having an optimistic approach to the teachings and perseverance from my Latinx immigrant culture, way of living and determination to reach "the American dream." Our *gente* never give up, le *echan ganas* until the very end.

Being able to contextualize the importance of perseverance and embracing our experiences to move forward and developing the lifestyles we want our life to consist of is one of the most radical acts of love towards ourselves. This for me is derived from the resilience of my parents to make sure we succeeded, from my their teachings at home instead of our socioeconomic status. Most importantly, it was in honor of my parents' journey, struggle, and dedication to ensure we had more options, so it had to be worth it.

Reflecting back at my younger years, my first promise to myself was that our household income would not be a determining factor for my future, nor that it would stop me from pursuing what I wanted to accomplish or experience. Though I was not sure what it would entail, now I have figured out how to live my best life. I feel free and connected to my most authentic self, more than ever before in my life.

At twenty-six, I am content with where I am. I have published my first book and am in the middle of translating it. I have pursued my education through different programs, and I have learned to value and love myself. I have learned that appreciating my body, mind, heart, and friends and family around me, attracts that same energy. This inner-peace was challenging to obtain. It required a lot of unlearning and relearning of ways to love myself and how I allow others to love me. I have learned to embrace that I am a blessing in the life of those around me, just as they are in mine. This has come with countless therapy sessions, alone time with dark thoughts to process and release. It has also included learning healthy coping mechanisms on my own and with professional support.

I service my community in the ways I can by being intentional of where I work and the spaces I partake in. Through my current place of work, I like to focus on situations of domestic violence and share my thoughts with survivors. I validate their experiences and thinking process, but I focus on guiding them to access the resources to obtain their liberation. I can live in my present, enjoy the beauty of life, nature, and others. Needless to say, I look forward to the journeys that are yet to come.

THINK YOUNG AND GROW

The key to living a life we love, is persevering through obstacles tossed at us. It is embracing the challenges, making the best of them and pulling ourselves together to reach a life we are content with. This can be accomplished through adapting an optimistic way of life, self-awareness and kindness. We can all use more healing energy, motivational friends, and nurturing spaces. We can all use less of negative or stressful situations

In our *cultura,* we are generally not taught to put our well-being first. My challenge to you is to put yourself first. Love who you are and take the steps needed to live a life you love, one that is fulfilling to you. Then, watch how you project a warm, compassionate and healing bright light and energy onto others. From the purest place in my heart, I ask, do you love yourself? Are you happy? Are you living or are you merely surviving? Be your own cheerleader, ignite your own spark. Don't be afraid to glow, grow and thrive—be excited!

THIS IS ME

My name is Michelle Nathalie Ramírez. In 2017, I earned my BA from DePaul University, with a double major in sociology and Latin American and Latino studies, and a minor in peace, justice, and conflict resolution. I am a trained interpreter (Spanish) and author of *Libérate: Moments of Strength & Perseverance* which was released in July 2020.

Currently, I service my community as a lead case manager family support specialist at one of our local nonprofits. In the upcoming months, I will start a mediation skills training at Dominican University, and hope to finalize the translation of Libérate. Soon after, I hope to work towards an MA degree in community social work. Whatever my future holds, I will bring it back to my community and will continue participating in advocacy and activism towards the well-being of my Cicero community residents.

The next ten years I hope are filled with growth, spirituality, and joy.

THE FIVE-YEAR PLAN

1. Traveling: Puerto Rico, Africa, and my home countries
2. Writing: New publications, have my books in class curriculum, community reading groups
3. Learning: MA degree, other certifications, fostering knowledge and growth

---

LIZMAIRI VARGAS

"Your love cannot belong to others if it is not felt inside you."

Life is only one path: destined to end, but a challenge to survive. It is that journey that sets each of us in different directions, but as we follow our given paths, we encounter distinct scenarios that shape who we are. Some experiences we are grateful for, but others we struggle through. That is just life, but as we grow up in this puzzling world that we have created, sometimes our true identity gets tangled. This story shows the revolutionary transformation of me, a little girl who kept her pain quiet when she was destroyed by humanity's standards; a girl who hated herself, but who used those same factors that pulled her down to bring herself back up. And this story, my story, starts with a sad setting.

BIRTH

On June 21, 2004, my mom, at nineteen years of age, had all the happiness of this world because she was about to give birth to a beloved daughter. Excitement began to pile up in her heart at the prospect of seeing and holding me for the first time. Unfortunately, that never happened. It only took seconds for her to close her eyes forever and not experience what she desperately awaited for months. After a fatal heart attack, I was immediately removed from her. Due to a lack of oxygen, my whole body turned purple. The doctors had to cut the umbilical cord inside an incubator, where I spent a full month in recovery after my weak birth.

It was a silent day in the town of Azua, in a southern province of the Dominican Republic, when my mother's death was announced. My mother was known on every block; people knew her as an extroverted person, number one at the school and always willing to help others. She was the person who would brighten every place she went with her smile. Knowing the story of my birth and my mom's death was hard, but as I grew up, everything in my life got worse.

I was raised in a small neighborhood, which I consider part of my family, with my mother's parents. My grandmother sent me to school at three because she always said I was a very smart little girl who needed to start her education at a young age. Throughout my education, students in my school would treat me differently, make me feel inferior and would look down on me. Sometimes, I would see a group of people and from the minute I would get closer, they would start laughing at me. Other times, they would change the topic of conversation, or simply stay silent.

Students often bullied me, making fun of how I spoke. Classmates referred to me as "the special girl." As time passed,

I thought they created that name because I was born without a mom. I heard their murmurs as they would secretly talk about what it was like to live with your grandparents. They would show disdain every time I mentioned "my mom who passed away," making rude facial expressions at me. I didn't understand why they did that. I wasn't the only person who didn't get to meet their mother.

At this time, I was a seven-year-old girl who didn't know anything about bullying or self-defense. I was exhausted every night thinking about why people treated me in such a way and why I felt betrayed by those I thought I could rely on. My early school years were traumatic. Even now, I remember being on the school playground and a classmate insulted a friend of mine. I confronted her in an effort to defend him. I don't remember all the details, but I still remember her shouting in front of everyone, "I am so happy your mom died." From that day, those words were tattooed in my mind. I didn't have the confidence to tell my grandmother what I was experiencing in school. After hearing that, I stopped caring about myself and just felt dead inside. All I experienced in those years was under an obscure cloud that trapped me, feeling nothing.

I tried to be like others so they could accept me. I typically found comfort being at home, but I started going out because that was what my friends enjoyed. I dressed and acted like others to fit their expectations, but trying to be like others was just another in the mistakes I was already making. Months passed and I was the same trapped girl, afraid of speaking out her feelings, but not even having an answer as to why I was afraid in the first place. My identity was already covered with a dark shadow that made me focus on the negative aspects of my actions. I did everything I could to make everyone happy because I wanted appreciation, but never received anything in exchange. I believed that by being like others I would stop feeling lonely.

FAMILY

My social life at school wasn't the only thing that made me confused with the world. I went through harsh moments that impacted how I developed my personality throughout my life on a daily basis. My aunt's unstable relationship was the only visual representation I had of love. I witnessed indirect domestic violence. My aunt's husband lied, cheated, and verbally abused my aunt, leaving a deep emotional instability and breaking the essence of who she was. My grandmother raised me alone at the time, so I thought my uncle's treatment towards my aunt was typical.

I remember my aunt, my two cousins and I being thrown into the streets after a huge argument between my aunt and her husband. My aunt stared at me with a broken heart, trying to look strong, but in vain. I was terrified. I expected a sleepover, but instead I had a shocking experience. After that day, I stopped believing in love. I had this idea that love was something only seen on TV shows. Love was like a flower in a crystal ball that could be broken with any stumble; it wouldn't last.

When I was a child, I saw my grandmother depressed

sometimes, and noticed her health problems get worse. The hernia which had formed when she fell days after she gave birth to my mother, would randomly hurt her. The sinusitis she developed from working in an industrial factory with strong fumes during her early years created severe chest congestion in her. My grandmother always told me that she was born with chronic anemia, and she wouldn't get to live many more years. I was constantly scared that the person raising me could die when any of these health conditions started acting up.

Being raised by only my grandmother was tough. My grandfather had moved to the U.S., and I only saw him once a year. He had left for the U.S. with the hope to bring his wife, his daughter and his soon-to-be granddaughter years earlier. When my mom passed away, my grandfather continued to pursue that dream. He found a job in New Jersey, and continued the legal process to bring my grandmother and me.

My biological dad took a different route. He planned on coming to the U.S., but when my mom passed away, there was an opportunity for him in Spain. My grandparents had known my dad since he was a baby, and the relationship between both families has always been strong. Even though it was a hard decision to leave his newborn baby, he knew that I would be in good hands. He legally signed papers for my grandparents to become my legal guardians. He would call a lot and visit me every year. I have always had an amazing relationship with my dad.

My grandmother was both my mother and father when my grandfather left to the U.S. and when my dad left for Spain. It was hard to see her sick every day. I would watch my grandma coughing with no limits, breathing through her mouth because she lost her sense of smell and using inhalers to feel better for a couple of hours. Suffering, but persisting through her own pain to focus on her role as a mom. I would watch her, and I couldn't do anything to help her, I didn't know how to. It seemed to me I was just not enough to help my grandmother with what she was going through. I was only eight, but I had experienced so much. Night after night, cry after cry, I would think and look for the answers to my questions: why were these things happening; why couldn't my grandmother be healthy; why was I disliked by society? But I never got an answer.

I lost hope of succeeding in life. I thought that I was the reason why my mom died. I was the reason for her heart attack. In my head I was a burden to my grandmother and a reason for her health getting worse because she had to put her time into me. Feeling like I was the reason for all the negative things surrounding my life led to one single phrase: hate. I hated myself for being me, for being different.

My great-grandmother was the queen of the Vargas family. She was diagnosed with Alzheimer's disease when I was five. She lost her memory and got skinnier every day. I remember my cousins being afraid of her because of how she looked, but I never felt that way. I would buy sponge cakes with jam at the supermarket (her favorite), and I would go sit with her every day at 4 p.m. and help her eat it. I was the only person she recognized while she was sick.

When she died in 2012, I was devastated. However, the sadness propelled me to think differently about myself. I noticed that when I spent time with my great-grandmother, I acted like who I truly was and not what people expected to see from me. I was the only person my great-grandmother remembered. I was important. And that single fact was the turning point in my life that shaped who I am today.

Sometimes people change their perspective on how they see life. That year was one of the most life-changing years I have experienced. My great grandmother's death made me realize that I was a unique person. I had a reason to be in life. She would smile and look deeply into my eyes. The connection I had with her sparked my interests to discover what I liked in life. It was during those months when I was eight years old that I saw every single negative thing—feeling like I was the reason for my mom's death, my grandmother putting her time into me, kids from school insulting me—and I finally chose to overcome those obstacles. My mom had to leave, but she didn't leave my grandmother alone. She left her with me so I could be the reason for her to endure her loss. My grandmother's health issues seemed to get better when I started to build a strong bond with her. School was just school.

REFLECTION AND SELF-LOVE

Those mean, cruel and harmful sayings from school did not stop immediately, but as I discovered this strong character inside me, I had the courage to confront these people. I stood up for myself. I started to surround myself with people who showed they had good intentions and stayed away from those that did not. Those feelings of not being enough made me push myself harder to prove I was wrong. Instead of being mad at the world, I looked for reasons to be happy with the world. Hate towards myself finally turned into love.

Learning to love myself was a process. I had to heal from a lot of mental and emotional pain that I had witnessed and lived through. I realized that "love yourself" means more than liking myself or feeling happy and calm. "Love yourself" is a bunch of feelings in one. I learned to admire myself, take care of my deep emotions, make time for myself, and be comfortable with who I was. This feeling cannot be described easily. When I learned to respect myself, all my actions began to describe who I am. In order to love myself, I had to let go of the past and not let the resentment take over me. It is fun to be different, because everyone is different. Everyone has something that no one else has in life, a soul, and that is what you should care about.

Now, when I see myself in the mirror, I see a very different person from who I was before. I am proud of myself for becoming me. I am determined to follow my own path. I am strong enough to keep fighting in this world, full of positive and negative influences. I see the person who I wanted to see inside me. As I grew up, I realized that all the obstacles I went through in life make sense because they were put in my life to make me better, to make me stronger and helped me discover who I was. This is my life and I should really appreciate the beauty of it. When my time to see in the right direction came, I knew what I did wrong in my soul; I was preventing it from growing the way it wanted.

God took my mother but left me, because I was meant to be in this world and my mom was meant to be by God's side. It is the same answer as to why anyone is in this world. From the moment the world was created, you were meant to be here because your soul is important. Listen to yourself. Cry if you have to cry and fight for what you want, but do it for yourself and not for others. Everything will eventually fall into place. You will be able to understand how to love others because to love somebody you must love yourself first. I had to learn to love myself for me to love back. Your love cannot belong to others if it is not felt inside you.

I am a miracle. I am an angel. I will become that woman that that little seven-year-old girl needed by her side. I have a bright future ahead of me. I always knew I had an amazing family who taught me the principles and importance of unity, but now I can appreciate it more.

Although I couldn't meet my mother, the happiness of being the daughter of Luisa Vargas will be with me for the rest of my life. I will work hard for my goals in life to create an impact on society by showing the world that you can do anything with your whole heart. I have met people that still try to put me down, but when I think about all the things I have accomplished, those people are set aside. I have obtained things in this life through hard work and through being myself. Life is too short to worry about what people think of you; you must do what you think is right for yourself.

THINK YOUNG AND GROW

Do you truly love yourself? Do you even know what it is to love yourself? I was stuck the first time I thought about these questions. If you feel the same, I challenge you to explore the world in your own way. Think about what things you would like to do, but for some reason don't try. Recently, I went hiking and I connected with the breeze of nature and felt the peacefulness within my heart. This experience gave me more motivation to improve myself.

I would like for you to try something new, something you find interesting. I encourage you to read books about self-motivation and being yourself. Try listing the things you want to describe yourself as. Practice those things you mentioned in that list. Trying something new will change your perspective of certain things in your life. This will help you find your true self. Do not let anyone take the happiness within you away. Focus on your values and desires and practice them. Then, the rest will happen naturally.

THIS IS ME

I'm Lizmairi Rosmery Vargas Santa. I am a sixteen-year-old Dominican girl. I came to this country six years ago to achieve what millions of people want: the American dream. I am a junior at Dover High School in New Jersey. In the future, I hope to become an accountant, not only because I like it, but to honor my mother who shared the same dream.

THE FIVE-YEAR PLAN

1. Become a marketing manager with a concentration in accounting

2. Help the hardworking and impoverished people in my country that my government forgets about, and build comfortable and sustainable homes for many

3. Buy my grandparents an apartment with an amazing view of the ocean in Santo Domingo

BEING THE FACE OF A LEADER

ANGELA CAMPOS

"Just by being you, there is someone you are inspiring."

My name is Angela Campos, and I am a student leader for change. Before you read my story, I would like to give some background about myself, a reflection of who I used to be when I was younger to who I am today. I am the youngest of six children to immigrant parents from El Salvador, a small country in Central America. When I was younger, I used to be very shy and reserved. Often, I would be too nervous to speak up and did not have confidence in myself. I never would have imagined myself as the person I am today.

Now, recall your first impression of a leader. Was it someone who inspired or motivated you? Was it someone from the dominant race of society or someone who was a minority? Now, when you think back to the first time you were in front of a leader, did that person look like you?

At first, these seem like simple questions that can be quickly answered. However, take a moment to really think about the first time a leader has impacted your perception and outlook on life. I saw society's leaders as people who were tall, had light skin with light eyes, and were mostly male. This was society telling me that leadership was not achievable by someone who looked like me. I was not fit for that role because I looked different. Being young, I did not think it would have a major impact on my thoughts or self-esteem, but it did. It developed the ideas and perceptions I had of myself, and I could feel society forming my place in its construction of a stereotype.

The perceptions and the stereotypes from society stayed with me throughout my education. I was fortunate enough to attend schools that were well funded and supported. The downside of attending these schools was that in some cases it supported society's views of myself and showed me how hard it would be to fight for a place I belonged. In my school, people who looked like me—those with darker colored skin, who identified themselves as Hispanic/Latino—were at the bottom, as we were attending a white institution. It showed me the downside of being the minority in a classroom setting, and feeling like I did not belong.

CONFORMITY

During my middle and high school experiences, I would surround myself with others from a similar background as my own, a protection mechanism. When my peers and I were together, we could truly be ourselves. We could talk in Spanish and talk about our culture and relate to one another. We did not have to conform or change who we were based on our surroundings. This allowed us to feel like there were more of us than there actually were. However, my peers were not always able to be around me. We would be together outside of our classes, such as in the lunchrooms and in homeroom. When heading to classes, it was a different situation. I was on my own. Being alone meant I was the only person of color in the room, where I would have to fight to be seen and heard because others treated me like my opinion didn't matter.

Often, I would find myself in situations where I didn't even recognize who I was. In my case, I found myself with imposter syndrome. At the time, I didn't know what imposter syndrome was. Now, I have learned that imposter syndrome is the experience of feeling like you are not being honest with yourself, like you have only succeeded due to luck and not based on qualifications. In my case, imposter syndrome was changing who I was based on my surroundings. I couldn't be my true, authentic self in the classroom setting and with other students who didn't look like me. I felt as if I had to change who I was in order to be seen and heard and succeed in my education.

I was constantly questioning who I was and wondering why I had to hide one of the most important parts of myself. I soon realized that I didn't have the same luxuries as some of my Caucasian classmates, luxuries like having parents who did not have struggles with helping you with classwork or understanding material. Not because it was hard, but because others were not fortunate enough to continue their education when they were younger. While others were in school, they were busy making sacrifices, where they would no longer be able to continue their education because they had to take care of their family and work.

My parents were not able to continue their education because they had to work at an early age in order to help their families. When my parents were growing up, my grandparents told them the importance of either working and helping out the family or continuing their schooling. Unfortunately, my parents were not able to choose both. Their families were not able to afford school, so working was the only option. They both chose to help their family by working. So, when I needed help with my schoolwork, they were never able to help. This made me realize that I was not as equipped as other students in my class, since they knew that their parents would be able to provide support because they had the background and knowledge from when they attended school.

These ideas, as well as others, began to develop my mentality at a young age, where I thought that I was not as equipped as others. This mentality told me that society did not and would not have faith in me and believe in my capabilities as I matured. I thought that no one would see me as a leader, a person to implement change, or be able to inspire others because that is what society taught me.

In high school, I had my first opportunity to be a leader and it was incredibly scary. At first when hearing about the opportunity, I rejected the idea, because I thought that no one would think of me as a leader. Although it wasn't a huge leadership role, it was the first experience I had that helped me evolve into my current leadership skills. The opportunity was called "junior leaders," where students would be a leader of a gym class of their choosing for the year.

The students selected would essentially be the teacher's assistant in regard to materials and paperwork, and assist the teacher and students in whatever necessary. After hearing about the role, I felt like I shouldn't try to take on the opportunity because society told me what a leader looked like, and that was not me. Per society, I was told that someone like me would never be seen as a leader, and that I was meant to stay at the bottom. So, when hearing of this opportunity, I didn't think I would be right for it.

This was truly disheartening, as it made me think that I was not good enough to be a leader, that I did not deserve to see my full potential. I thought back to those moments where I felt like I did not belong, and that I would have to change who I am in order to fit the ideals of others. I thought the only way that I could be a leader or be seen as a leader was to fit the "look" of society's leaders already displayed. As a result, I was not as comfortable showing people my culture as I am today. At times, I felt shame showing the pride I had for my culture and all that was unique about it. I didn't want to be seen as not fitting in to the "ideal" society and those who fit in it. I thought I would need to change others' perception of me in order to be seen.

STEPPING OUTSIDE MY COMFORT ZONE

When I entered my undergraduate career, I was excited to finally have a change. Many people say that your college experience is the time when you easily see and meet people just like you, that it is so easy to be yourself and be comfortable in your own skin. In my case, it wasn't so easy. I picked a school that was a predominantly white institution. I was the minority there once again. I was at the bottom again, exactly as society had destined.

At first, the transition was hard, as it would be for any college freshman. It wasn't just hard because it was my first year of my undergrad, it was hard because I felt like I didn't belong, like I was out of place. I felt I had to fight to feel I was worthy enough to attend my own institution.

Being a minority during high school was very challenging, but continuing that mindset into my undergrad experience was harder than I could have imagined. During my first semester at my college, I already felt like I didn't belong. My first indication was not being able to find many students who were from a minority background and maybe that were the first in their family to attend a higher education institution. I knew that it would be challenging coming into an environment like this, but being in this situation, it was something I could never have imagined.

I had several situations that happened to me, and others that made me feel like we didn't belong. I had gotten used to usually being the only person of color in my classes, but continuing this in higher education was different. I heard comments said to me and other classmates saying degrading things based on the color of our skin. I also heard and felt microaggressions during this time that made me question my abilities—and myself. Hearing and seeing these microaggressions turned my world around, because I thought that situations like this might have stopped during my undergrad, but I was wrong.

I had situations where faculty or staff would question my past in regard to my ability of being fit or worthy enough of pursuing my education. I had one situation where a staff member questioned my ability in my major because they did not think I would be able to be successful in that profession. This staff member told me that I should switch my major, because he thought that those similar to my background typically struggle in this profession. At times, I didn't know if this was on purpose or by accident, but in my mind, I thought, "Would they have said the same thing to someone who wasn't a minority?"

One day in class, we were discussing the topic of higher education and how everyone is capable of succeeding based on their background. My professor talked about how there are usually some instances where those who come from a diverse background may not always succeed, that those who are typically minorities are less likely to succeed. She then proceeded to ask the class if they could think of any reasons why minorities are less likely to succeed in higher education or if the class could share any personal experiences. After asking, she looked right at me. Then, other Caucasian students looked at me to see if I would say anything.

As I was too nervous and confused to say anything, another student stated that they believed that minorities are less likely to triumph in higher education because they usually have more obstacles, but mostly because they do not belong in higher education. My heart dropped. I couldn't believe that someone could have the nerve to say minorities didn't belong in higher education, especially as I was sitting right there in the classroom. There was no hesitation or remorse. For them, this was a fact, not just an opinion. I already felt like I didn't quite belong at my school based on the color of my skin, but hearing this made me question things even more. I had to work harder and fight to show them that I *did* belong.

As a result, I felt like I made a mistake by attending a predominantly white institution. I thought, "How could I have been so dumb to pick an atmosphere that would essentially place me at the bottom again? How did I pick a place that made me feel out of place and not give me the courage to make me feel that I could become the leader I wanted to be?" The situation did not make me feel comfortable enough to showcase who I truly am, and how could I allow myself to do that.

These thoughts were very hard to deal with, as was not being able to find those who looked like me. I thought it was going to be easier based on a preview day I had attended before committing to the school. During this preview day, it was evident that this school did not have many Latino students, so that made me hesitant. But one counselor who was the same background as me discussed that there was still a good population of Latino students on campus. With this in mind, I decided not to think too much about the race of the student population, because I needed an institution that would best help with my learning ability. When coming to campus, I thought it would be easier to find those Latino students, but that was not the case. It was so hard to find people from a similar background as my own, and to find leaders who looked like me.

But then it happened. In the middle of my first semester freshmen year, I found students with a similar background, and to my surprise, there were more than I thought. It took getting out of my shell and being uncomfortable to find them. I heard of some organizations on campus, but as a freshman, it can be really scary to be in a new setting with a new organization. I went to my school's Latin American Student Organization (LASO), and after a few meetings, felt more comfortable and more at home. I was able to connect with students in LASO because most of them were Hispanic/Latinos and were first generation students. The students in this organization experienced similar hardships, being in a predominantly white institution. This allowed me to build connections and feel more connected to the school.

Through LASO, I got to meet some of the most influential and inspiring leaders my age. I found what society told me was not possible and not common. I discovered society was wrong, because there were young leaders here who looked like me, who were in the positions that I typically saw other people hold. I found the people who urged and encouraged me to take on a leadership position because we need more leaders who look like us. Not only did their leadership skills inspire me, but their character as well. Their drive for helping others, their ambition for a higher education, their sense of pride in their culture and their heritage stood out and inspired me. They showed me that Latinos are able to do anything that we put our minds to. We are able to become leaders while continuing to get inspiration from others and do not have to change who we are or where we come from to be seen as a leader. The pride and the culture that these Latino leaders expressed and showed to others was the fresh breath of air that I needed.

I got a firsthand look of what society told me did not exist. I saw strong Latinos who had pride in where they came from and did not hide it from anyone. When there was not a seat at the table for them, they made sure to pull up a chair to make sure their voice was heard, because it mattered. They inspired me not only by their words, but by the pride they had for their culture. They showed that *"I am here, and I am speaking my voice. I know you see me as a Latino, as a minority, but that gives me power."* These people inspired me to have confidence in myself and to achieve things like them. They gave me the courage to show off my culture and be proud of it. As well as the confidence to show off my Latinidad, especially because others in my school do not see it often. To not be afraid to blast my Spanish music, to speak my language, to show that I am a Latina. To be a leader. To not listen to what society has told me in the past, or what others will say about me now, but instead to lead for change and a better tomorrow.

BECOMING A LEADER

I am fortunate enough to have numerous role models in my life that have helped me develop into a better leader. From those I met in LASO, to a new staff member at our institution who is one of the only women of color in higher power, to family members who showed me what it means to be a leader, I know that Latinos are meant to be in leadership positions, and that we deserve to be seen as leaders. I know I am capable of inspiring others while finding myself inspired.

Coming into my undergrad, I thought I made a mistake by choosing a predominantly white institution because it would not help me grow into who I wanted to be. However, that wasn't the case. Although there were challenges, my institution did help me build myself into the leader I am today. I discovered there is power in being seen as the minority. I wasn't afraid to show my pride and authenticity—especially because it was needed.

When I walk into a room where I am the minority I say to myself that although I am the minority in this room, it does not make me less important. It doesn't make me less of a leader. I tell myself that the fact that there is no one else in the room who looks like me shows me the importance of my presence. I know that when others see me that they see my color. I recognize they see my color and that I am a minority, and that gives me strength and power by staying true to myself and my culture, to help me be a leader.

As a result, my experiences have allowed me to develop into a person I never dreamed I would be. I learned how to speak up and get involved. I joined numerous organizations in order to develop my leadership skills. By the end of my sophomore year, I was able to attain leadership roles, such as a resident assistant—meaning I would be in charge of a whole floor of first week students—and President of ALAS (Advancing Lives, Advancing Students), which is an organization developed to help mentor high school students in the surrounding schools. I also continue to serve as an active and contributing member on the executive board of our Latin American Student Organization. I am also a member of Gamma Alpha Omega Sorority, Inc., our first multicultural sorority on campus.

These experiences have helped me develop into a better leader, one where I can inspire those around me, while constantly finding myself inspired by the courage of others. I have gained so much more confidence in being a leader. I know that I have the capability of taking on leadership positions and making change for the better. I am no longer afraid to be myself in these positions, which has resulted in me being able to inspire others to be themselves. I am not afraid to speak of my culture proudly, listen to various types of Spanish music (even if others may not understand) or speaking in Spanish without feeling guilty. I am proud to pull up a seat in leadership positions, especially if there is not one available, so I have to make one. I have learned to not change or conform to fit the perceptions of others. That the differences and ideals, values, strengths, talents, history, and perspective I bring is the change that is needed.

I tell my story because I feel that it can relate to others.

It can relate to those who may be skeptical of attending an institution where they will be a minority. It can also be for those who are unsure how to show their true self, are feeling the reality of imposter syndrome, and are scared to show who they really are.

Even if you feel skeptical in attending a predominantly white college, know that your presence is needed to make a difference, to make a change for a better future. You deserve to be in any institution you choose, and should not let anyone make you think otherwise. If you are experiencing imposter syndrome, know that you are worthy of success. Do not doubt yourself. Life gives you many opportunities, you must be bold enough to take a chance and land on your dreams. To those who are scared to show who you really are—don't be. Be your true self. Showcase your culture, because it is important and must be celebrated.

If anyone tells you that you aren't a leader, that could not be more wrong. Everyone can be a leader, whether you have an executive position or not, whether you believe it or not, it's true. I guarantee that there is someone who sees you as a role model and looks up to you. Just by being you, there is someone you are inspiring.

It took a lot for me to realize my worth and become a leader. I hope to inspire others and those who were like me, those who did not see leaders who looked like them growing up, and were told by society that they did not fit the leader "look." Society and others have said that you are meant to be at the bottom. You are not. You are capable of being a leader. Your culture deserves to be brought out in your character as a leader. Our culture and history are beautiful, and must be brought to the table. So, I urge you to be your authentic self. Show who you are. Be proud in all you do. You are a leader. Whether you believe it or not, it's true.

THINK YOUNG AND GROW

I challenge you to go out and be the best leader you can be. Being a leader does not require you to have a position or have a particular leadership role. All it takes is to inspire others and work to make a change for a better future. I urge you to be the most authentic self you can be in everything you do. Do not conform or change to please those around you. By doing this, you will inspire others to not be afraid and be who they truly are. In addition, get outside of your box and experience new challenges and new hardships that will help you flourish as an individual.

When in a leadership position, be your most authentic self because you never know who you will inspire.

THIS IS ME

My name is Angela Campos, and I am the proud daughter of immigrants from El Salvador. I currently attend Carroll University, a small private institution, where I am double majoring in Spanish and public health to improve the future of my Latino community. In all I do, I hope to better my community, but also inspire the next generation of leaders.

THE FIVE-YEAR PLAN

1. To complete my master's degree in public health and continue work in leadership roles in order to create a more equitable life for those of a similar background to my own

2. Become successful in my career and continue to influence others to achieve their dreams

3. To travel the world and experience new cultures

THE POWER OF HAVING A VILLAGE

SUHAILLY VEGA

"I am a strong woman because strong women and a man raised me."

My story begins at the young age of six, when my village began to collapse. The environment was tense because my parents were going through a rough custody battle for my brother and me. My parents were never married; however, they lived together for several years. I had four other half siblings from my mother's side, except for Elvin Jr.—he was my full brother. I was the youngest.

My siblings and I lived with my mom in Elgin, Illinois, since I was born. While living with my mom, we must have moved four to five times. I was never given a reason why we moved. As for my dad, he owned a home after he separated from my mother. After a decade of working as a casino dealer at the Grand Victoria Casino, he was laid off. He sold our home and moved into an apartment complex.

My parents worked. My mother had her day job, and my father usually worked the second shift. My dad would pick Elvin

Jr. and me up on the weekends and sometimes during the week to spend time with him. However, my other siblings' fathers were not in their lives.

Growing up with my five siblings was quite fun and challenging. My sister assumed the role of a mother when my mom wasn't around. My brothers always watched over Elvin Jr. and me since we were the youngest. We didn't live an ordinary life.

As a young Latina girl, growing up without my biological mother by my side was not considered normal. In Puerto Rican culture, it isn't common that a mother is not in the picture. Mothers are typically the ones who stick around and give unconditional love. They would probably skip a meal or two just so you and your siblings could eat or sing "Sana Sana, Colita de Rana" when you fall. But I didn't have that. I grew up feeling that my mom was not capable of loving or caring for me.

NEW BEGINNINGS

When I was eight years old, the court gave full custody to my father. At first, it was hard to comprehend that my father would be the only one raising my brother and me. It isn't usual that a man would raise two kids by himself. The example I had of what I considered a perfect family was my father's extended family, consisting of a mom and dad raising their children together. I wondered who would comb my hair like my sister did or advise me on "girl" things. During this time, my dad decided we would move to Aguada, Puerto Rico, where he grew up.

As I strolled across the sad and dull hallways of Chicago O'Hare airport, I took a glimpse back in hopes of seeing my mom. My face was soaking wet with tears. As I embarked, I felt the chilly air hit my face as I continued to sniffle. After a five-hour flight, I arrived at my new forever home. I was yet again hit with a change of atmosphere. As I was escorted to the significant red EXIT sign, I felt my lips beg for water. The warmth and humidity invaded my soul as the Spaniards invaded our ancestors' land. It took me whole and drowned me in sweat.

Our transition to a new environment was quite challenging at first. Celia Cruz, a Cuban singer, would often say, "Ladies and Gentlemen, My English is not very good-looking." I could say my Spanish was not very good-looking. Not knowing the island's native language was a challenge. For that reason, my brother and I were enrolled in the best bilingual school on the west side of the island, Escuela Regional Bilingüe Antonio González Suárez. My brother and I were scared that we would not hold our own at this new school. There was a process of interviews and admission tests. After undergoing what felt like a never-ending process, Elvin Jr. and I were accepted. I could now say, "Ladies and Gentlemen, My English and Spanish are very good-looking."

Growing up with my father was amazing. We had wonderful experiences that led to new opportunities, which we wouldn't have had if we hadn't moved to Puerto Rico. He always took care of my brother and me, and made us feel safe. His transition to Puerto Rico wasn't easy either. He knew it wouldn't be easy for us due to the new culture, language, and environment. He had given up everything to give my brother and me a new life. He found it quite hard having to come to the island empty-handed and not being economically stable.

Coming from the city life to living on an island was very different. I went from hearing the constant noise of traffic and feeling the cold snow during winter to hearing the coqui, Puerto Rico's native frog, and going to the beach. Living on the island had a different rhythm; everything felt much slower and more relaxing. Growing up in Puerto Rico was wonderful. My family would explore the island's beauty, such as Cueva Ventana in Arecibo to Castillo San Felipe del Morro in Old San Juan, Puerto Rico. The best thing about living on the island was that we would go to different *chinchorros* (small outdoor restaurants) to eat on Sundays. We would also have picnics at the beach.

Even though I was excited to move to a new place, I was scared because I was 2,049 miles away from my mother. Despite being only a phone call away, I barely heard from her, which made me feel gloomy. However, I began to realize that I was not alone after all. I had so many powerful Latina women guiding me through life. The women in my life had come together to create a village where I felt loved and accepted.

A VILLAGE OF WOMEN

My sister, who was more like a mother at the time, was the first person who showed me love. She would always comb my hair and tell me how loved I am. She later became a mother herself at the age of eighteen, when I was four years old. As a child, all I could do was cry. She moved away to start her own family, and all I felt was the pain when I saw her go.

My father's mother, grandmother Nilsa, or as I like to call her, Grams, and my great-grandmother, Abuela Margarita, taught me how to cook. I consider them two of the best cooks out there. From *arroz con gandules* (yellow rice with pigeon peas), a staple in every Puerto Rican home, to *pasteles* (Puerto Rican tamales), they showed me how to cook all their recipes. They would always tell me the secret ingredient was love, and that the food was not the same without love.

The first woman who introduced me to the world of fashion and makeup was my father's sister, my aunt Meledy. I chuckle every time the memory of her dyeing my hair comes to mind. I was thirteen when my aunt decided to give me a makeover. Like any other girl at that age, I was excited about my new look. Having purple strands of hair sounded fabulous. My father was not on board with the idea of the spontaneous makeover. Once my aunt had finished dyeing my hair, her words of comfort were, *"Más vale pedir perdón que permiso."* I don't recommend asking for forgiveness instead of permission, but it did work for me at the time.

Even though she was the diva of fashion, she was also the person I went to for advice when I was bullied. When kids would bully me at school, she was the one I confided in because I saw her more like a big sister rather than an aunt. During those tough times, she helped me by giving me advice, not only as a teacher or an aunt but as a mother herself.

Many other women contributed to making me the person I am today. For example, my cousin Gisenia taught me how to eat eggs and toast together. Tía Forita showed me how to wash my undergarments by hand so that they would last longer. Cousin Marilynn taught me how to bake yummy desserts, like cookies.

Every woman that has been in my life inspired me in many ways, but the person who has inspired me the most is my cousin Jeanette. She is my father's cousin; she is a strong, hard-working woman. I look back on when I was a child, and all the memories I have with her are good ones. She has always instilled in me to do good so that good can come my way.

Jeanette is a co-author of *Today's Inspired Latina Vol 3*. Her story is titled "Childless is Not My Narrative." When I read her story, it broke me knowing that she and her husband could not have kids of their own, but little does she know I have her engraved in my heart as "Mama Jiny."

Together, we have experienced amazing things like traveling across the United States to visit the Mall of America, being tourists in Chicago, and shopping at Plaza las Americas in Puerto Rico.

Mama Jiny also took me to get my first driver's license. I will always cherish the little moments, such as when she gave me lessons on how to parallel park, going shopping, watching movies, or even the time when she let me take the Mercedes for a joyride. Every moment spent with Mama Jiny will forever be in my heart.

However, I still wondered about my mother in the United States. From the moment I arrived in Puerto Rico in 2009 till

May 2018, I only spoke to my mother a handful of times on the phone. It wasn't until Elvin Jr.'s United States Marine Corps Boot Camp graduation in May of 2018 that I heard I was going to see her. I was seventeen years old when I saw her in the flesh for the first time since leaving Chicago.

It had been nine years since I had seen her. I was going through a roller coaster of emotions. I started feeling excited because I was finally going to be able to see her and sad because I didn't know what to expect when I did. Our first encounter was in front of the hotel where she gave me a small gift, we spoke for about ten minutes. The next day, we all gathered for the graduation and had dinner together. Being able to have my family together—mom, dad, brother, and I—made me happy. I wished the moment didn't have to end.

A PATH TO HEALING

After seeing my mother at my brother's graduation, I decided to try and re-establish a relationship with her. I returned to Elgin, IL, on July 3, 2020. At first, I planned a two-week vacation, but I stayed for six months. My first semester of college was switched to online due to the COVID-19 pandemic; I decided to stay to continue working on our relationship.

When I was boarding the plane to Chicago, all I could think about was finally being able to have that mother-daughter time I always desired. So many expectations and hopes filled me. It would be my first time staying with my mother alone, without my father and siblings present.

As I was disembarking the plane, flashbacks of my eight-year-old-self came to mind. I remembered the airport halls and how cold they felt. As I kept walking, my heart started beating faster and my palms began to get sweaty. I felt like I was invading a stranger's land, my mother's territory. I looked up to take a glimpse of my mother; this time, she was there waiting for me.

I ran to her and hugged her. At this point, it had been two years since I last saw her at my brother's graduation; I hoped and wished my mother would be swept away with a sea of emotions. As she wrapped her arms around me, I got the feeling that she was a little tense and hesitant. It made me feel a bit uncomfortable.

During the six months that I lived with my mother, I got to know her more. I learned that she doesn't like watching telenovelas and that she cooks really good Mexican food. She also finds it peaceful when she visits her mother's grave and bring her flowers.

While staying with her, I asked her many questions about her childhood and my grandparents. At first, she was reluctant to answer my questions. She eventually told me that her parents were not the type to show physical affection towards her and her siblings. She continued to say how hard-working her father was and, while he worked, her mother stayed home to take care of ten children. Yes, ten kids!

People often say that you are the product of your environment, and I didn't honestly believe it until I heard my mother's story. It makes sense the lack of attention towards Elvin

Jr. and me. I can understand that maybe the way she was raised had to do with how she turned out to be. She was not accustomed to receiving love or affection. Therefore, I can see why she wasn't affectionate with her children.

She later told me that her family moved from Puerto Rico because the farm owner where her father worked passed away, leaving my grandfather without a job. They needed a source of income, so they moved to the United States. My mother was a teenager, and it wasn't easy for her to assimilate into the American culture, much less the language. I could relate because when I came to Puerto Rico, I had to learn the language, customs, and traditions. However, I was able to assimilate to the Puerto Rican culture because of the village of extended family on my dad's side.

Being raised in an unaffectionate environment wasn't helpful in my mother's upbringing. She didn't know anything but what she learned as a child. I am grateful for having the opportunity God gave me to spend six months with my mother. It gave me a lot of insight into who she is.

As for me telling my side of the story to my mother, I had planned on telling her during my stay, yet I couldn't find the right moment to express my feelings towards her due to us not having much alone time together. However, all I can hope for is that she picks up this book one day and reads my story, and no matter how indifferent it may be for her, she gets the chance to understand my story.

As I reflect, overall, I'm happy with my life thus far. I have overcome my childhood and teenage years! Moreover, I got into one of the most prestigious universities, the University of Puerto Rico, Mayagüez Campus. Now that I'm older, I reflect on how I was raised and by whom. Once I moved to Puerto Rico, many women were instrumental in making me the person I am today.

The indigenous group, Kraho from Brazil, says, "We should all be raised by many mothers." They believe the children should have a more independent life and their own identity. I can say I have a sense of self-worth and self-respect, which makes me a strong woman, because strong women and a man raised me.

THINK YOUNG AND GROW

Who outside of immediate family members have had the greatest impact on your life? Who makes up your village? Which women empower you to do better? It's important to know who makes up your village. The people in your life can positively or negatively affect you; they can either make you survive or make you thrive.

THIS IS ME

My name is Suhailly Vega. I am a Puerto Rican, born in Elgin, Illinois. I am currently pursuing a bachelor's degree in psychology at the University of Puerto Rico, Mayagüez Campus. I am an active volunteer in the nonprofit organization The Autism Hero Project. I dream of having a successful career, getting married to an amazing man, and starting a family.

THE FIVE-YEAR PLAN

1. Doctoral Degree in clinical psychology

2. Become a lawyer

3. Have a home of my own

LABELS: A RESTRICTIVE IDENTITY

CELESTE LEON

"My differences are my light. I won't hide myself to be accepted."

It was my senior year of university and I was entering my fifth interview for my first potential "big girl" job. That morning I wrote down with much enthusiasm:

"My differences are my light. I won't hide myself to be accepted. I will show up as I am—with my values, my story, and what excites me. I have worked hard to be here. Intention and authenticity are key aspects in who I want to become."

I was one of the five people in my university department to land a job with a Fortune 500 company—a dream that once seemed so farfetched for a young immigrant Latina, the one with an accent, the one that always felt like an outsider, and the one who doubted her worth too many times.

As we grow through life, we all develop unique personality traits and ambitions. However, many of us grow up to believe that our differences are a weakness and feel pressured by society to conform with trends to be liked and accepted in order to achieve a hierarchal position in society that we think will keep us safe. By the time I was thirteen years old, I had lived in many countries and cities that constantly made me realize how different I was from those around me. In my world, I couldn't understand why I always felt like an outsider in every classroom I walked into. I inherited the belief that having an accent or having widely different perspectives and ways of living was shameful. This is because I was focused on the wrong thing.

MY STORY BEGINS

I was born in a tropical city of Peru called Piura. I grew up with a large, loving family, many friends and a powerful connection to nature and our ecosystem. When I was five years old, I moved to Montreal, Canada. Montreal is the second largest primarily French-speaking city in the world, after Paris.

During my years in Canada, I learned French and realized there are many cultures that the world is composed of. This was my first experience of acculturation, the dynamic process immigrants experience as they adapt to a new country, which is not easy. Moving to a new country is scary because you have no network, there is a new lifestyle you need to adapt to, and it takes you out of your comfort zone. Because I was a young girl, I adapted and embraced my time in Canada. I realized that the world was a lot bigger than I thought—people spoke different languages, they dressed differently, and valued different things. To have been exposed to this lesson so young was powerful, but I didn't truly put this together in my mind until I was a bit older.

When I was eight years old, my family decided to move back to Peru. During the next two years, I moved to different cities within Peru and attended different schools. Subsequently, my parents divorced, and I moved to the capital, Lima, to start a new school year hoping to have more stability with my father's family. As I started my new life in Lima, I realized that I felt very different from my peers. I had to work on my Spanish again from my years away, and I realized my childhood travels were unique to others, often making me feel like an outsider in the country I was born in, which sparked my insecurities to grow stronger.

I remember that some of the first things that made me self-conscious were my calcium deficiency and my eye birthmark, especially because relocating meant reliving these experiences again. At eleven, I still had seventy percent of my baby teeth because they had not fallen out naturally. As a result, from ages eleven to fourteen, I went through multiple surgeries and there were times where I had missing teeth while I waited for my adult teeth to finally come down. During this time, I would never smile, and I would try to speak in a way that would cover my teeth from showing as much as possible. When I laughed, I would cover my smile with my hand so people would not see my missing teeth. I felt embarrassed. I also had a large birthmark in my sclera, the white part of the eye that surrounds the cornea. Whenever I met someone new, they would stare at my birthmark and sometimes harshly ask if it had an eye tattoo, a birth defect or just what was wrong with me. I couldn't hide my birthmark because it was in my eye, and these were constant reminders that made me feel like I needed to hide.

These experiences began to plant doubts about who I was in my mind, and I found myself repetitively observing my surroundings to understand how others communicated, how people perceived others, and what certain actions meant within the community. As children, we are constantly having new experiences and interpreting what they mean. From going to a new school, learning how to play with others, understanding how to behave properly, and more, we develop a unique personal lens that gives meaning to our lives. Eventually, we create a perception of our world—of what is acceptable or unacceptable, common or uncommon—which can be dependent on where you are in the world, and often becomes how you judge people or events in your own life.

At thirteen years old, I moved to New Jersey with my mother. I was ready and excited to learn about the culture, make new friends, and be the best I could be to succeed for my mom. By now, I had already experienced multiple relocations and knew that if I was going to make the most out of this experience, I needed to work hard and take responsibility. My first goal in America was to learn English, and within a year, I was able to communicate with those around me. I joined the soccer team and began making friends. After my first full year of schooling (eighth grade), I received A's and B's and got involved in the community, which gave me a little more confidence in my abilities.

However, during this time, people would often make fun of my clothes and my accent. I had a unique style compared to other Americans, because I came from a different culture, and I began to realize that many times as I walked down the halls, people would stare me down and whisper things to one another. This made me feel like an outsider, as I focused on how different I was to kids around me, but I continued on in my line.

I saw many people get discriminated against for having accents, too. When kids made fun of my accent, it made me feel like I needed to speak less, and pushed me to think that people didn't like accents because they were too different. After years of people making fun of my accent, my mind began thinking that my voice mattered less than those without an accent or those who had been born in America.

Consequently, I turned to the media to understand how people like me, Hispanics with accents, were portrayed in the United States. First, I began to realize how underrepresented Latinos were in film or media, and how strong the stereotypes were highlighted in the few instances I did see representation. Latinos are still subjected to parts that play into the stereotypes of the cop or the criminal, the illegal immigrant, the maid, or the emotional sex kitten. In addition, these stereotypes are also perpetuated through the news media.

All this information shocked me, especially because I was born in South America, and have firsthand experience with the abundance of culture, vibrant people and success stories that exist in our Latin Heritage. The many labels that Hispanics had embodied through media and film made me feel confused and scared, because I did not want to be labeled like the stereotypical Hispanics portrayed in the media, when we are so much more than criminals, illegal immigrants, or sex idols.

LABELS

During my teenage years, I searched for labels and societal cues to tell me who I should be as I struggled with my identity. This created a lot of internal fear, which made me shy and stopped me from putting myself out there. I diminished and criticized my authenticity many times to be liked and feel accepted by those around me because I didn't understand my own value. This external comparison between the world and myself had immense power over me, which made me struggle with self-worth and confidence for a long time. Eventually, this confusion is exactly what pushed me into my self-discovery journey of "who do I want to be" and this began by changing the labels the world, or my own mind, had given me.

Living in many cultures taught me that each culture has its own frame of reference—a sharing of reality that gives people within a particular culture common knowledge, shared traditions, ideas of foreigners, labels, and specific behaviors that are often different from other collections of people, such as how you were raised or what is the role of a woman. This helps us understand our communities and create order during communal interactions. However, this also taught me to be aware of my inner culture, what I believe in, and what I stand for, and as such, I can honor myself like I respect the cultures I encounter, too. My next step was to understand what labels are and how our perceptions of these can change.

A label is a descriptive word or phrase that gives information about the object that it is attached to. Neurologically speaking, labeling is a good thing—it allows our brains to make sense of the world so we can navigate through it easily. However, when we use labels to describe people, it has a more profound effect. Labeling theory states that the labels applied to individuals influence their behavior, because people come to identify and behave in ways that reflect how others label them. Particularly, using negative or stigmatizing labels can promote deviant behavior, which causes feelings of confusion, being misunderstood and can create internalized separation from the rest of society. George Herbert Mead, an American philosopher and sociologist, explains that the self is socially constructed and reconstructed through the constant interactions each of us has with the community. Thus, if the community labels an individual, eventually, that individual will integrate this label into his sense of self.

I began to learn about labels and how people construct their identity around nineteen. I wanted to empower myself with knowledge because I often felt like I was the only one experiencing these doubts and internal battles, so I knew I needed to get out of my head. Learning more about labels taught me a big lesson in my path—we are meaning making machines, and the meaning I create from my experiences and the words I hear have a huge effect on my mental health. What I believe about myself and my experiences will shape my day-to-day mood, the way I treat myself and the opportunities I pursue. Despite having these multiple insecurities from my teeth, my different styles, my accent, and more, I realized that I had a purpose—to succeed for my family, to make myself proud, and to be a positive influence for those around me. Therefore, I couldn't let these factors stop me from achieving my dreams. I made an agreement with myself to work through my insecurities, one day at the time, through self-development and education, to rise above and become the woman I always dreamed I could be.

The first step in letting go of labels was understanding how my experiences shaped me. I had to further understand how my multiple relocations and my parents' divorce had affected my psyche. According to the University Hospital System of Northeastern Ohio, moving and experiencing a parents' divorce are in the top five traumatic events in life. This new awareness pushed me to begin journaling and working towards becoming more self-aware.

Second, I had to understand how people making fun of me—the way I dressed, my accent and my cultural differences—had affected the way I presented myself to the world and how the words of others had now become my own internal negative voice. This pushed me to question the stories I was repeating in my mind and work towards more empowering and loving self-talk. I now understood that because I had not seen a plethora of positive Latino representation, the stories I had created in my head such as "people like you don't often succeed" did not serve me and I could not let that stop me from creating a version of me that I had envisioned with so much hope. The labels I had acquired—not growing up in a stable home, being a child of divorced parents, being different than those around me and being an immigrant with an accent—all had a meaning in my head that came from the outside world, which does not represent who I am and the wisdom I have learned from these experiences.

The third step in letting go of labels was creating a future version of myself that I admired and could work towards. Often, we go through life waiting for luck to knock on our door, but real changes occur with intentionality and vision. On May 6, 2018, I opened my notepad on my iPhone and started writing down things that make me passionate, what type of woman I wanted to become, and the impact I wanted to create. The woman I dreamed of is confident and courageous, she exudes love, wisdom, and vibrant energy, and strives to make a positive impact in her community through her hustle, her interactions and her creative outlets.

Labels can provide a restrictive identity as they can make you think that this is the way you are, and you cannot change. We often become the labels that society gives us and let it be the driver of our lives, but to hold on to labels is to cut your own wings.

I have been consciously working on deconstructing my labels and identity since I was nineteen. I was able to graduate from Monmouth University with summa cum laude honors and land my first job with a Fortune 500 company here in New Jersey.

I recently passed the four examination parts of the Certified Public Accountant (CPA) Certification, some of the hardest exams I have ever taken in my life, because I am creating the version of me I envisioned. In addition, I am the co-founder of I AIM Community, an empowering space for women to create a better relationship with themselves and dream for more through educated discussions, sisterhood, and a support system. This experience has forced me to speak publicly regularly, reinforce in me that my voice matters, regardless of the accent, and be courageous with my vision.

Embracing my accent and my self-expression has also been a part of the process of stepping into my power in my journey of self-love. I used to think that because English was my second language, I would never be good enough to communicate or inspire others. However, by pushing myself, writing regularly, and journaling, it has helped me communicate more effectively and taught me how to better untangle my thoughts into coherent sentences. Writing is a skill that must be practiced, because most people aren't born with perfect communication skills or with the ability to express their inner world to others precisely. Furthermore, in writing there is no accent, and you can control the narrative without the external forces of nonverbal communication and biases to how we look or speak, which is a more authentic expression of our inner being.

COURAGE

Courage is the second step in letting go of labels because

you must be willing to stand up for yourself and reframe your perspective when others may use labels to bring you down or assume things about you that are not true. If I want to show others and myself that I am more than the labels I may be perceived as, I need to stand tall in my light and be courageous in order to be a walking representation of what I believe in.

When I was sixteen years old, I first learned what a CPA was through my friend's mom. She spoke highly of her CPA and that is when my curiosity in this career path began. I began to ask her questions and show my interest. However, she described how challenging this career is, and insinuated that I was not capable of achieving such success by telling me that this wouldn't be a good fit for me. Maybe she assumed this because I had only been in the U.S. for three years at that time and was still adapting to the society. Therefore, I wouldn't be capable of accomplishing and pursuing this career, but she didn't really know me. She didn't know my story, my determination and my hunger for growth.

There will be many people in our lives who doubt us, diminish our potential or label us as incompetent or unmotivated. However, the courage to bet on yourself when others don't is an empowering skill that can keep you going during hard moments. Learning to harness the strength within yourself to validate your emotions, your experiences and your dreams will create a better relationship with yourself, give you more courage to pursue your passions and take more risks to create the future you desire.

Even if you have not moved to as many cities as I have, you may have still felt like an outsider at some point in your life.

Whenever you try something new, such as a new activity, habit or a new business, you may be the minority in a group of experienced people. You may feel like an outsider. This feeling may regularly come back because growth is a never-ending process. We often wait to achieve a certain goal to give us permission to think we are finally worthy. This is a trap. Your difference is valuable, and no matter where you are in your journey, you are worthy and you have the ability to create beautiful things and experiences on this Earth.

We can prevent the effects of labeling by limiting social shaming and embracing more tolerance of differences. However, this must begin with ourselves. When we finally embrace our own differences, it is when our internal door opens to treat others with that same kindness and tolerance. As we get older, we may meet people of all religions, races, genders, sexualities and political beliefs. The effects of working on this can help us create better relationships with others in the long run, be a leader in our communities, and use our differences to make a difference. I've learned that my differences are my light, and my difference of being is what I teach to others.

THINK YOUNG AND GROW

The most powerful change begins with ourselves. I invite you to change the labels the world has given you through further understanding of how you acquired these labels and what they mean to you, through harnessing the courage of your why to fight against those labels and lastly, to accept yourself for those differences that may have been seen as negative once but could be your superpower today. We are all imperfect, but each of us has unique strengths, desires, and vibrations.

The better you get to know yourself, the better you can showcase your strengths. It is not necessarily a matter of how others see you, but how you see yourself in your most loving and authentic self. As you begin to be true to yourself, you will shine bright and attract like-minded individuals. Work on your belief systems and be intentional about your growth. Be proud of who you are and always continue learning, because you never know who you could become. As you go on with life, find people who will support you and encourage you to always be a better version of yourself. Create safe spaces for others to express themselves free of judgement, and embody what it is like to not hold yourself to limiting labels.

THIS IS ME

I am a Certified Public Accountant (CPA) at KPMG LLP and the co-founder of I AIM, a self-development community for young women to grow into greater versions of themselves and make a greater impact in the world through educative discussions and a support system. I am passionate about community building, mental health, and financial literacy.

I was born in Peru and have lived in four countries, including Peru, Canada, England, and the United States, and I'm a fluent Spanish speaker. This experience has allowed me to expand my perspectives and ideas of who I am in a unique and beautiful way, which drives my love for poetry writing, working on myself, and sharing my light with others. For more information, you can find me at www.celesteleon.com

THE FIVE-YEAR PLAN

1. Start a podcast based on empowerment and growth

2. Start an organization that helps people in their financial journeys with tools and knowledge to grow their wealth

3. Write a poetry book

MELINA TIDWELL TORRES

"My hope in life is to continually find ways to inspire the people around me."

It was a beautiful September morning as I stepped out of my mom's car that day. I walked into the foreign building with sweaty palms and a racing heart—my first day of high school. A new school, new friends, fourty-five minutes from home; away from everything and everyone I knew. It was my first time being brave and taking charge of my own life. For the first time, I was creating my own path.

Before that day I had gone to my town's public schools all my life. I lived in North Arlington, New Jersey, a small town where almost all of the students stayed in the public school system from pre-k to high school. Only a handful of students in my middle school were applying to private high schools at the time, let alone applying to more than five different schools. Making the decision to start looking at private high schools was not something ever suggested to me by my guidance counselor or teachers, and certainly was not done by many students in my public middle school.

My mom was the one who first introduced the option to go to a private high school. She knew that I had always excelled in school, and saw in me the potential to do more. There was a time when I loved my school and the friends that I had in my town, but that love had begun to disappear. My mom's words of encouragement really allowed me to foster the idea that I could do more, be more, and strive to be my best self in and out of school.

With that in mind I applied to A Better Chance—a program for students of color to prepare for high school entrance exams, interviews, and the application process for many of these institutions. I was fortunate enough to be accepted and began tirelessly practicing my interviewing skills, studying for entrance exams, and writing supplemental essays for my applications. It was not an easy process by any means, taking up most of my free time outside of school and dance.

Between schoolwork, dance classes, and high school research, my free-time dwindled as did the number of friends who wanted to hang out with me. As high school acceptances were released and other classmates got wind of what I was doing, many were rude to me, assuming that I thought myself better than them because I no longer wanted to go to school in town. The end of the application process was bittersweet. On one hand I had been accepted to some of the best high schools in my state, but on the other I felt more alone than ever before. Scattered friendships. Alone on my own path.

I struggled to find the confidence in myself and the decisions that I was making. I found myself engulfed by perpetual sadness and anxiety, and at the time was unable to articulate these feelings to anyone but my diary. The loneliness of eighth grade year consumed me and led to suicidal thoughts and severe panic attacks. By the time I had reached my eighth grade graduation, I felt empty, only putting up a fake smile when need be. I couldn't see it at the time, but my choice toleave school in North Arlington would be life changing for me.

THE ROAD LESS TRAVELED

I feel as though my life can be perfectly described by Robert Frost's following quote, "Two roads diverged in a wood, and I—I took the one less traveled by, and that has made all the difference." In the past six years of my life I have found myself constantly traveling down paths that no one I knew had traveled down before—not my family nor my friends. From the minute I decided that I did not want to attend my town's high school, I began carving my own path in life. It was not always easy traveling on paths less taken—and even at times creating my own path—but I do not think I would be my authentic self if I had pursued the paths that my friends and family urged me to follow.

The building that had at one point been foreign to me, became my home for the next four years. My time at the Academy of the Holy Angels was transformative. In the beginning, my days consisted of school and dance. Being a part of the Holy Angels Dance Team was one of the most significant parts of my high school experience. Months before my first day of high school, I tried out for my school's dance team, made the team, and immediately began working. From that moment on, every day was a dance day. As a team, we had practice six to seven times a week and practiced for hours after school and then would have to make the fifty-minute drive home afterwards. With the dance team in my life, there was usually never much room for anything else. However, something inside me itched to do more.

I knew that I wanted to do more than just school and dance. I always had a passion for service, volunteering, and finding new communities. Although I loved the routine that I had created, I wanted to be more involved within my high school outside of just the dance team and academics. On top of dance, I joined my school's Student Council and Angel Ambassador Program. By the end of my freshman year of high school, I juggled going to school, going to practice, and participating in club activities.

Just when I thought I was busy enough, I stumbled upon a club called Operation Smile at Holy Angels. On the promotional flyers for their meeting, I saw a young child with a lip condition; I found myself intrigued by the flyer so I decided to attend their informational meeting. During that first meeting an upperclassman presented her experience as a student volunteer on an international medical mission. I sat mesmerized and moved by the girl's experience and all I could think in my head was, "I want to do that."

For the next three years, I got myself more involved with Operation Smile at Holy Angels. I helped to fundraise in and out of school, and then eventually decided to become involved with the larger organization's international student programs. I attended a high school conference for Operation Smile in Rome, Italy, during my sophomore year, and there developed an even stronger passion for the organization and its mission.

During my junior year at Holy Angels, I decided to apply for medical mission training, but because of my busy dance and academic schedule I did not put in as much effort into my application as I should have. This resulted in my rejection from mission training for that year. I knew in my heart that I wanted to one day participate as a volunteer on a mission, so for the next year, I focused more of my time into our school's club and continued to develop my relationships with members of the international student programs of Operation Smile. I went on to become co-president of our Operation Smile club my senior year and decided to reapply for medical mission training during the next cycle. I was finally accepted in December and by the end of March 2019, I was blessed with the opportunity to travel to Zunyi, China, as a student volunteer on an Operation Smile medical mission.

It was not an easy task by any means trying to fit everything I wanted to do within the twenty-four hours we are given each day. It became an exhausting balancing act at one point: managing my academics, dance, family, extracurricular commitments, and the service activities that I wanted to do. I was balancing it all, or so I thought. I found myself missing a crucial component: my mental health.

If there's anything that I would go back and change today, it would be the lack of focus that I had on my mental health. At the time I did not know much about how fragile and precious our mental health is. I never gave much thought to the panic attacks that I would have, or the deep sadness that would consume me at the end of my days, or the anxiety I felt standing at the back of the dance studio. What I learned over time was that there is no such a thing as a perfect balancing act. I failed. Many times at that. I came to realize and accept that I could not be the perfect student, perfect dancer, perfect volunteer, or perfect volunteer all at the same time. All I could do was my best. In everything that I did, I put my best foot forward. If I did poorly on an exam or was rejected from a program, I would not let it destroy me, instead I would reevaluate how I could do better going forward.

IVY LEAGUE

I made another life-changing decision my senior spring of high school: college decisions. For four years, I worked hard in and out of the classroom. I spent endless hours in the dance studio training, studying at home for my classes, and volunteering in and out of Holy Angels. During the application process, I felt confined by the guidance counselor's urges to apply to what she deemed "safety schools" for me. But what was stopping me from applying to some of the best universities in the country? Why should there be even an inkling of doubt in my abilities to work hard and be successful? In my mind, the worst thing that could happen was that I would be rejected, and if that happened, so what? So, I gathered the courage and applied to over a dozen universities.

In March 2019, as I sat in my hotel room in Zunyi, China, my mom called me frantically letting me know that I had been accepted to Brown University! I was the first person in my family to be accepted to an Ivy League university. No one from my high school had attended Brown in the past few years, let alone a student of color. I had accomplished what at one point I thought was the impossible. I was one of the 8.5% of students that had been accepted to one of the most elite institutions in the United States. There had been a time when I sat in my bedroom in middle school praying that I was smart enough to get into a private high school, now I was an Ivy League student.

The summer transition between my senior year of high school and freshman year in college was filled with a lot of self-reflection and growth. It was the first time in a long time that I found myself with absolutely no commitments. I took this time to practice yoga and meditation every day, go to the beach, and focus on my physical and mental needs. I pulled my knowledge of meditation from my high school religion classes and took the time to actively find moments of stillness, reflection, and relaxation. Over the course of that summer, I incorporated meditation and yoga into my daily and weekly routines. By the time I left for my first semester of college, I felt refreshed and reinvigorated to begin a new and exciting chapter in my life.

My first semester and a half of college was one of the most amazing times in my life. It was my first time away from home, meeting new people from around the world, taking classes that I wanted to take, and experiencing life as an adult (well to some degree at least). During my first semester, my mom presented me with a new opportunity: an application to be a speaker at Young LATINATalks Northeast. Having begun a new chapter in my life at college, I was looking for new communities to become a part of, and the thought of collaborating with a group of Latinas made me so excited! At first, I was hesitant. This opportunity was something completely new to me; I was not a professional speaker by any means, but I took the risk and applied for the opportunity. A few months later, I received an email of acceptance to the event as one of the eleven speakers, and it marked the beginning of my immersion into a community of beautiful and strong women.

FINDING A BALANCE

At the peak of my freshman year, life came to crashing halt. The coronavirus pandemic put the entire world on pause. The year of 2020 changed so many things for everyone across the globe. For me personally, it stunted a lot of the self-growth that I had made from the summer of 2019 into my first year of college. It halted many of my pursuits and goals that I had for myself academically and extracurricularly.

That year became one of the biggest obstacles that I had ever faced in my life. It was a time of complete isolation that forced me to dig deep and find the light at the end of my tunnel. These unusual periods of complete stillness can be easy traps for depression and sadness. I would be lying if I said that I did not find myself trapped in there for a while, but this time of stillness allowed me to slow down and reflect about my life in that exact moment. I was able to prioritize what was truly important to me: my physical health, my mental health, my family, my education, and the service I was able to provide to others.

The year since the start of the pandemic has been a constant battle between happiness and sadness. Feeling as though I am constantly trying to overcome obstacles in my life and keeping a positive mindset has not been easy, but I am appreciative for the moments when I am able to find happiness and peace.

Throughout the pandemic, journaling became a way for me to process my thoughts and feelings. Journaling had always been an escape for me; I have always kept a diary or journal of some type ever since middle school. The emotions that I struggled to express vocally, I expressed on paper. It was not until the beginning of my sophomore year of college that I took the step to reach out to a therapist at my university. Over the course of 2020, I learned more about the importance of mental health and working to destigmatize its conversations within my friend groups and family. I was able to find people to talk to openly, allowing myself to be vulnerable, and opening space for my loved ones to be vulnerable with me.

My hope in life is to continually find ways to inspire the people around me. That is the reason why I have chosen to share my story with you. Life is not easy, and there are endless paths that you can take in life, but it is important to choose the path that will lead you to your most authentic and genuine self. In the past six years, I have learned a lot about myself and reflected many times on the journey that I have taken. I feel blessed to have had all of the opportunities that I have experienced in my life. Behind everything that I have done, there have been hours of hard work and dedication put in. The path to where I am at was not easy by any means, but I would not trade it for anything else. Alongside with the sacrifices, obstacles, fatigue, and loneliness that I felt at times, these darker moments are overshadowed by the immense happiness, success, and fulfillment that I have experienced over the years. As I continue to go through Brown, I live my life the same: working hard, putting passion into the projects I do, and surrounding myself with things and people that make me smile.

It took a very long time for me to develop confidence in myself and the path that I had created for myself. There were periods of time where I felt completely alone. There were times when I was completely unmotivated. Before I knew about and practiced self-care, there was one person who kept me going: my mom. She was the one who initially suggested that I find a different high school. She has pushed and supported me from the very beginning. She believed in me every step of the way, even when I did not believe in myself. She has been my rock through it all. She continued to remind me even throughout the darkest periods of my life that I had a life worth living and was destined to do great things with it. She helped me find the happiness in my successes, and find the motivation and confidence to continue on the path that I had paved for myself.

THINK YOUNG AND GROW

I now challenge you to take time to meditate and reflect. Ask yourself these questions: Are you happy right now in this moment of time? Is there something you can do to make sure that you are happier tomorrow and in the future? What active steps can you take to live a happier and more fulfilling life?

It does not matter if you are fifteen or fifty-five years old, it is never too late to change paths and pursue your dreams. Never let anyone or anything stop you from pursuing a path that draws your attention. Be brave and be willing to make a big leap in your life. The world is filled with opportunities waiting to be taken. Find the confidence and courage within yourself to make yourself happy, and to make the changes that are necessary for you to feel fulfilled at the end of the day. Taking these steps to creating your own path may present external and internal obstacles, but with self-confidence and the right support systems, you can achieve anything that you set your mind to.

THIS IS ME

Hello! My name is Melina Tidwell Torres, and I am from a small town in northern New Jersey. I am half African American and half Ecuadorian. I grew up dancing and went on to win two national championships with my high school dance team. I currently study at Brown University as a public health concentrator and am pursuing medicine. At Brown, I am a part of several clubs, including the Afro-Latinx Alliance. I am also the founder and president of Operation Smile at Brown, a club that works to advocate and raise funds for children with cleft lip conditions around the world.

In the future, I hope to become a facial reconstructive surgeon in order to operate on children with cleft lips and palates. I would love to travel the world and visit different countries and communities, helping to spread change and health innovation. For now, when I am not focused on school or on my academic extracurriculars, I am in the gym working out, or trying new food! I've always had a great passion for athletics, and although I no longer dance, I have found new outlets for my athleticism. Coming from a diverse upbringing, I have always loved and continue to love trying new foods and restaurants.

THE FIVE-YEAR PLAN

1. I hope to be accepted into medical school after Brown

2. I want to explore what the world has to offer by traveling to new countries and immersing myself in their culture

3. My biggest goal is to make my family proud in everything that I continue to do

CELESTE GARCIA

"We need to approach life through a growth mindset lens."

I grew up in a Mexican immigrant household, in a suburb of Chicago known as Chicago Heights. As early as four years old, I remember my parents and grandmother sharing stories about the motherland, reminiscing on their experiences of struggling with economic hardship, which led my family to migrate to the United States—my mother as a teenager and my father when he was in his late twenties.

I grew up hearing stories of their experiences in Mexico. My family grew up struggling economically, and they often shared how they were grateful for the opportunities they had in the U.S. They held onto this gratitude firmly, even though they were undocumented for the majority of my life. Being undocumented meant they did not have access to the same resources U.S. citizens did, were more susceptible to discrimination in the workplace and not being properly compensated, and lived in fear of deportation, which led to the possibility of having our family ripped apart. I watched them as they struggled to hold jobs that provided living wages due to their documentation status, and had to endure many negative experiences.

Residency or *papeles* would open up so many opportunities for my family, but not having that guaranteed, I grew up feeling a sense of responsibility to fight for a path forward for us. For me that was through obtaining an education, which my parents instilled in me could be a transformative experience. Knowing this and having the privilege of being a U.S. citizen, I grew up feeling a huge sense of responsibility to honor the sacrifices of my parents and be able to advocate and provide for my family someday through obtaining an education. I knew that my American dream was to fight for the life that they fought for us to have, and not take any chance to do so for granted. They did not have access to the same opportunities I did—being born in this country alone was a privilege in itself—so doing well in school was a must for me. I always knew if I was going to reach my goal of breaking some of the barriers that my mixed-status family was facing, I was going to have to be serious about school. Better yet, I was called on to dream big and hold on to my vision. As early as eight years old, I wanted to be a lawyer and wanted to advocate for undocumented immigrants and their civil rights within the legal system.

FEELINGS OF OTHERNESS

With this huge sense of responsibility, there came a feeling of needing to be perfect. At the age of eight, I had concocted a simple plan: I would excel in school and be a stellar student, continue to do this for the rest of my life and I will earn my way into being an immigration lawyer someday. This is exactly what I did for a while. Through hardships at home, bullying at school, and all of the things in between, I held onto my vision and tried my best to not lose focus of my goals. I wanted to fight for a chance to see a crack of light in what felt like a hopeless situation at times. After all, I had to make it someday, I thought, to fight for a chance to change my family's situation.

In elementary and high school, I worked my hardest to be that "star student"—the student who had excellent grades and was a part of the honors programs, while also being involved in volunteer service and extracurriculars, sports, and holding leadership positions. Although it was not easy, I managed to keep this up and expected near perfection of myself in everything I did. Something I started to notice, however, was that my peers did not seem to have this sense of responsibility or vision. It was difficult to relate to them in many ways once I noticed that my family's situation was something that was not common. My parents had already shared that this is not something you share in public, but in addition this "family secret" made me feel more isolated, and like I was the only person going through this. I was shy and timid growing up, more intentionally than not. I felt like the fewer people knew about me the better. So I kept it a secret and kept working hard.

By the time my senior year rolled around, I learned that I would be graduating in the Top Ten of my graduating class (number six to be exact). My teachers jumped to congratulate me and assured me that I was to have a promising future in college someday. Despite having worked so hard all of these years, I felt like I didn't deserve the things that were coming my way. College acceptances, being uplifted in my community, scholarship money—was it just that simple?

From one day to the next, all of a sudden I had an open door that would propel me into a different universe. One where it felt like my parents and I couldn't co-exist. I would go on to college and just leave them, with the continued uncertainty of their future, while mine solidified and morphed into something that would cause us to continue to have fewer things in common. In addition to having felt very isolated from my peers, I started to feel even more distant and isolated from my family, which made this process more bitter than sweet.

Although I was so close to accomplishing the first part of my American dream, I struggled to navigate the college application with my parents' documentation status and being unfamiliar as a first-generation college student. I went from having dreams of attending Harvard University to just needing to successfully fill out one college application. This part of the process alone made me feel like the voices stemming from my imposter syndrome were true. It wasn't until years later that I identified these voices as imposter syndrome, which is an internal belief that you are not as competent as others perceive you to be. These voices told me I didn't belong on a college campus, especially when I couldn't even figure out how to successfully apply to one. Furthermore, I knew that my parents were not in a position to assist with the financial cost of college, which also added to my doubts. These self-doubts and the fear of rejection kicked into high gear, which led me to say no to several opportunities.

One of those opportunities was an internship that I got offered at a law firm my senior year as a result of a "fake" practice interview that seniors do as a requirement to graduate. The person that volunteered to interview me on that day was so impressed with my involvement and approach to the interview, she reached out to my guidance counselor and told her to offer me the opportunity. Although I was so excited when I heard about this, those feelings quickly were overcome with anxiety and worry. How was I going to be successful in this, if I did not know what an internship consisted of? I knew nothing about law and, therefore, I thought I would be a horrible intern. How could I possibly be an asset in this law firm? I reached out to my counselor and said yes, but did not show up on my first day. My decision to let that opportunity go was embarrassing and soul-crushing, but through this experience, I learned that the cost of letting my fears and doubts win was greater than allowing myself to try.

Things started to take a turn once I started finding community and articulating what I needed help with. Although I had done things on my own for a while, I felt I was at the point where I needed an intervention. To my luck, I was approached by a recruiter from my local community college—the first Latina that I had met working for higher education, Jennica. She saw me roaming the halls of my high school one day and seemed eager to know what my college plans were. I felt embarrassed not having a solid answer, but I lied and said I would be going to a private institution and was ready to take out loans. I thought this would shoo her away, but instead, she had this alarmed look on her face and advocated for us to have an in-depth chat about my college plans.

From then on, Jennica worked with me one on one to learn what my situation was. When I finally admitted to her that I didn't know how to fill out my FAFSA due to my parents' documentation status, she assured me that she would help me fill it out and there was a solution to that. I instantly felt like a weight was lifted off my shoulders. I felt so lucky that someone saw my specific situation and was able to connect me with the information and resources that I needed to make the best decision that I could for my family and myself. As a result, I ended up taking a step that I had never imagined.

After a few sessions with Jennica, I registered to attend my local community college. It was difficult for me to accept at first, since it was not my ideal result walking away from high school. I had all sorts of insecurities, about whether I would be able to still accomplish my professional goals. In addition, I had heard all these stigmas around attending a community college—how it felt like an extension of high school, and that there were little to no opportunities to grow and get that college experience. I had one teacher even encourage me to take out loans to go to a private school in Chicago. "If you stay in Chicago Heights, you'll never leave," he said. As others were making the case against a community college, I was rather disappointed in myself for being in this situation. I felt so far removed from someday accomplishing my professional goals in the future.

Having so much to consider and with the guidance of Jennica, I decided that attending a community college would be the best financial decision for my family and I. Although it was not the decision I envisioned myself taking after working hard in high school and having dreams of going to an Ivy League school, I realized that at least getting my foot in the door of a higher education institution was just as monumental as going to a prestigious school, especially since I was going to be the first in my family to have the privilege of doing so. Luckily, I had been playing volleyball during high school and managed to land a volleyball scholarship at the college as well. Often things in life don't go as planned, but we have to trust that with a lot of hard work and prayer, things will work out in our favor in the end.

FAILING FORWARD

As I was trying to get over feelings of not wanting to be at a community college, I was immediately struck with difficulty navigating college life. I would soon find out that there was also a "hidden curriculum" or norms in college that aren't explicitly discussed. These included: meeting with your professor during their office hours to build a relationship and ask questions, reaching out to professors for extensions on assignments, and that there were resources on campus like emergency assistance funds for students with unexpected financial expenses, and ways of getting cheap (or even free) textbooks.

The first semester took a lot of adjusting and when I received my first-ever final grades for the semester, I was devastated. I had bombed almost all of my classes and my GPA was very low. It was so bad that my volleyball coach sat me down to have a conversation about potentially losing my volleyball scholarship if my grades were to continue this way. This felt like a new low point for me, and I had serious thoughts of dropping out. Aside from my disbelief in my ability to succeed in college after I tanked my first semester, people around me were telling me to quit and just work, *porque no era buena para eso.*

One day before the deadline to enroll for another semester, I remember sitting there and thinking of my options. Both the thought of moving forward with school and trying to pick myself up academically, mentally, and spiritually seemed like an impossible task, but quitting on my dream of someday becoming a professional and supporting my parents and myself seemed just as painful. I had to come to terms with the fact that if I was going to succeed (graduate college and then become a professional) I had to accept that success was going to look a lot different. Things didn't turn out as I hoped for, and I couldn't possibly imagine what was to come at this point, but I would just take it day by day.

I decided to enroll for the second semester. I knew that I was going to have to make many changes in my life and be very serious about coming up with strategies to succeed for the next semester. However, I did the work. I showed up to tutoring, started following up with professors during office hours and asking questions, and I even formed some of my study groups. I was still involved on campus and even had a part-time job, but I meant business.

I also had to make the difficult decision to distance myself from people and situations that didn't align with my goals and values as well. Day by day, I reflected on what I could do to position myself closer to where I wanted to be and tried not to get discouraged by what other people thought about me, my potential, and my ability to persist. Most importantly, I tried to push the doubts I had internalized, for me to pull through I had to believe that I could.

As time went on through the year, I started finally getting the grades that I knew I could, and as I did, I became more confident in my academic and leadership abilities. I started viewing this as a huge growth opportunity for myself and learned to give myself grace in this process. We need to approach life through a growth mindset lens, knowing that if we are not great at something, we do have the ability to improve and should give ourselves space and patience to do so.

GIVE YOURSELF PERMISSION

Though I learned many things through this experience, one of the greatest lessons has been to allow yourself the room to try something new and expect yourself to fail. Not only is it in our nature, but failure allows for an opportunity for you to learn more about yourself and lean into your strength. Additionally, you need to know that you are worthy of your dreams despite feeling like things are not supposed to work out in your favor. I used to be embarrassed about how I had struggled to get to where I was—now I embrace it and understand that it is part of my own story that will someday inspire someone else.

It was with true disbelief that I held a letter in my hands, sent to me by the President of the community college, saying I was set to graduate in May of 2015. It was a congratulatory letter notifying me that I was one of three students that would be awarded the President's Award for Excellence in Scholarship and Leadership at commencement, and would graduate while being seated on stage as a distinguished graduate. I had thought about all of the odds that were against me during my two years at the college, and how at one point I was considering walking away and dropping out, out of fear that I would not make it through.

Earning my associate of science would be my first college graduation as a first-generation and low-income student. As I reflect on my journey, I think back to all of the things that I was able to go on to do after graduating from a community college that would not have been possible if I had quit early on. I would be offered several jobs after having shared my story of persistence with employers, which surprisingly made me a more marketable candidate. I would later go on to transfer to a four-year university in Chicago, where I would win the chance to moderate an event interviewing Ana Navarro, a prominent political figure for an evening event in my school surrounding the current political climate.

Also, I would go on to be a mentor to several students at the university and community college I attended, being able to serve as a resource on how to connect to resources on campus and strengthen their study strategies. I would later graduate again with my second college degree, a Bachelor of Science, and see my parents' faces light up when I dedicated my degree to them for all of their sacrifices and hard work to provide for our family.

My career trajectory was the accumulation of exploring different majors and playing with the idea of different careers in college. By the time graduation came around, I landed on wanting to work in higher education, working alongside first-generation and/or low-income students through support services to connect them with tools and resources so that they can find their path towards success as well.

All of my experiences put together have opened my eyes to the work that needs to be done in education to make the systems equitable and socially just. This passion has led me to work at several institutions, including doing national service through AmeriCorps at Northwestern University and a year later, working at Purdue University Northwest with their TRIO Upward Bound program. This program offers high school students special workshops and seminars regarding careers, college admission, financial aid, tutoring, mentorship, and all the things in between regarding college readiness. If this is something you are interested in, I highly encourage you to look up the program near your area, or reach out to your high school guidance counselor for more information.

As a young Latina, I encourage you to keep your mind open to what the world has to offer you; and if you're spiritual, for what God has to offer you. There is a greater purpose for our ups and downs, and I've realized that my journey has positioned me with the passion to give back and someday inspire the next generation to keep going. By being a part of their journey, hopefully I can aid in unlocking their greatness.

THINK YOUNG AND GROW

Fear and self-doubt are both symptoms of imposter syndrome that can affect us and stop us from tapping into our full potential. Take a moment to reflect on the opportunities you are interested in pursuing or have been thinking about creating. Write down all of the skills and qualities that you bring to that space—do not hold back! Keep these in an area that is easy to reference and refer back to them when you are starting to doubt yourself. Remember, you do not need permission from anyone but yourself to try something new and give yourself space to learn and grow. Making mistakes is a part of the journey—embrace it!

THIS IS ME

My name is Celeste Garcia. I am passionate about providing support and mentorship to first generation college students. In my current role at Purdue University Northwest, I serve as the outreach coordinator for the TRIO Upward Bound program. In my spare time, I like to play volleyball, go hiking with my family, read memoirs, and do anything outdoors.

I aspire to continue to serve first-generation students in higher education and/or through nonprofit organizations. My ultimate dream is to create a nonprofit that serves first-generation/lower-income students in the south suburbs of Chicago through enriching experiences, mentorship, academic, and financial support for college access.

THE FIVE-YEAR PLAN

1. Create a video podcast platform, where first-generation Latinx students can gain insight on the different challenges that they may face in higher education

2. Delve into higher education and journalism, and find where these two fields overlap

3. Obtain a master's degree or an advanced degree in public policy or education

NICOLE BARAJAS

"My happiness is up to me, so I won't let my emotions control my actions."

In life everyone has a story to tell. Every story reaches a climax point. At that point we have the option between a yes or no that can change your life forever. You have the power in yourself to choose the way you want to let your emotions control you. We get thrown these wicked curve balls one at a time, thinking, "Why do we go through so many obstacles? But do we think about the positive outcome? A lesson learned, new experiences that come our way. That yes or no question will pop up in our life more than once.

Ever since I was a little girl, I have always been outspoken and had a vivid mindset of what I expected from life. I was one of those kids that had to have a plan for everything, but as I grew, life did its job and put me on my path, where I went through moments in my life that I learned lessons from my experiences, this included meeting individuals that have inspired me through their own struggles and success. Let us be thankful to have those people in our life for giving us a helping hand as we navigate the wonders of life.

A PAST BUILDS A FUTURE

I was born on December 9th, 2000, to a teenage immigrant mother from Durango, Mexico and a first-generation Mexican American father. I grew up in a predominantly Latino community in the Chicagoland area named Pilsen, from the time I was born until 2005. At the time, the neighborhood had a high crime rate and my mom didn't have much work experience, so my father decided to move us to Garfield Ridge for better opportunities.

Growing up in a close *familia*, our values of dedication, passion, love, strength, and faith in God are what fueled my ability to take on life. Thankfully, my parents had the help from their families. Love was always there for me, but one person that made every day a bit better with a hug or a home-cooked meal was my "mommy Rosie." When I think of the strong warrior she was, she inspired me to push through in all my battles. Even though she had many illnesses, she never lost faith in God, in herself, and the power of prayer. I am the woman I am today because of her teachings. I remember her putting my sister and I in the kitchen at a young age to learn new things, from a traditional Mexican dish to the spices we would use. Throughout my childhood, I didn't notice, but she was preparing me for the day she left this world.

From a young age, I was able to always catch on to certain

feelings if they were off. This feeling always kicks in when something bad was going to happen. To this day, this feeling has been my secret weapon that has helped me prepare for these situations.

When I was twelve, my parents decided to split up. My mother took my sister and I to the town of Aurora, IL, to live with our grandparents and aunts and uncles, where we all lived in the same house. Before this I lived with my father's family, where I was able to experience having my nana, "mommy Rosie," live with us, and our house was where everyone got together for the holidays. My family has been my backbone and my biggest critic. Having a tight family comes with its perks and flaws. For one, you're never alone and always have company, but, on the other, your decisions are always dictated. Once my parents divorced, that meant only seeing my dad's family on weekends or holidays; I went from seeing them every day to only a couple days out of the week.

As the years went by, I got to experience two sides of family love. The way my mom's family expressed love was different. At a young age, I wasn't able to understand why they were not affectionate like my dad's family, or why my grandparents didn't say "I love you" as often. This was a big reason why I didn't feel close to my mom or her family. Knowing that I had to live with them made my weeks very long, because I missed having my loud, crazy, blended family. By the time Friday came, I would get so excited to see my uncle Jorge in the truck waiting to take us back to the city. I missed sleeping in my old bed, enjoying my nana's food and getting to see my extended family after Sunday mass. Then it was back to Aurora for another week.

As I entered middle school, I knew it was my time to *begin* my journey of trying to find myself. The moment I knew that I needed to go live with my dad was when high school counselors came to give us our schedules and give us a tour of the high school. I was scared of starting a new school and didn't really have guidance at home, since my mom was always working. At fourteen, I didn't know if I was making the correct choice, so I enjoyed the tour and took in all the great activities I could have taken. Sometimes I felt that I wasn't going to be able to handle a big school. Oswego East High School felt like a mini university to me, with all the buildings and facilities. When the counselors gave us a sheet selection of classes I took it back home and asked my mom for help. I could tell that she was tired from work, so I kept it to myself until that night that I called my dad to let him know. He helped me out picking honors and AP classes to get started with a good balance. I don't blame my mom for not being able to help, because I know she was facing her own storms while trying to figure her life out. I appreciate what my mom was able to do, but I felt as if my mom felt obligated to take care of Destiny and I. She was young and trying to form a new life. I couldn't understand the feeling before, but I was angry at her for not being so involved in my life.

In middle school, I didn't get much support from my mom. We would often end up butting heads, arguing about the homework, or not having the patience. I remember crying in the closet thinking why does my mom have us living with her? Is this to get back at my dad? Since their divorce, thoughts like that would come in and out of my head. Even though we were living with my mom's family, it felt very lonely, since it was just my sister and I on our own all day, until night when mom got home. Sometimes I would get homesick and felt that I didn't belong there, frustrated that I couldn't live with my dad. Those moments I would debate if I should tell my mom I wanted to go back to my dad, feeling uncertain and scared of what my parents' response would be. I was scared of being punished for wanting to go back, or not being able to see my dad. Through my last year of middle school, I debated when the right time was to finally tell mom that I wanted to go back, feeling anxious as I thought of her response.

The summer before high school started, I got to spend three months in Mexico as my eighth grade graduation present. Towards the end of my trip, I had a Skype call with my mom and dad about me going back to Chicago. My hands were sweaty and I felt nervous, messing up and mixing Spanglish as I spoke. I was scared that my mom would say no to moving back with my dad. I could hear her voice crack with sadness and tell me that she wasn't going to stop me from going back, that I was free to go if I wanted to. In that moment I felt joy that I could go back, but sadness because I was leaving Destiny alone. But it was time to head back to Chicago to start a new chapter.

AGAINST THE CLOCK

As I walked into my first period Algebra class, I began to wonder what I was doing here. Other kids just looked at me and began talking among themselves, pointing their fingers at me. This was just like the first day of middle school, I had the option to let my emotions take over me in a positive or a negative way. I embraced who I was and didn't let their opinions bother me. A social butterfly was in the process, as I started to get along with classmates from all classes.

Throughout high school, I did the best I could to succeed in all my classes. I reminded myself that I was going to make a name for myself to show that a kid from any background can achieve success by dedication and persistence. My dad encouraged me to then take all honors classes to get my GPA high from the start. He was setting me up to succeed. I remember feeling as if we were preparing for battle, as I prepared to get myself through school and into college. This was where my dad started to put more pressure into my high school experience, expecting top grades, extracurricular activities, multiple service projects, and excelling in every activity I joined. At fifteen, it felt more like work than school, but I loved it. School was my happy place.

Freshman year at Kennedy High School was one of my best years. I was in a mixture of regular and honors classes, which allowed me to meet people from different backgrounds, different races, and different mentalities. This was an influential change in the way I got to experience meeting new people and new mindsets, due to my old classmates in Aurora being of

Indian, Jamaican, Filipino, and white backgrounds. Going back to Chicago, where my neighborhood's demographic was mostly Latinos and whites, influenced the way I saw life. In high school I got to meet people from different upbringings, and whether through food or dialogue, I got to learn something new.

At first, I didn't know if I wanted to join any clubs or sports. Then, one day my P.E. teacher asked me to join her water polo team. I was scared and nervous, but thankfully, there were some classmates of mine who I knew that were going to join. I decided to try something new. This was the beginning of my best of memories, meeting my closest friends, and finding out who I was becoming as a person.

Sports changed my life for the better, because it was the first step I took toward loving myself. Making that choice to wake up at 5:00 a.m. every morning to go to practice was always one of the first steps I needed to feel good about my day. Being there in the water allowed me to clear my mind. Before practices or games, I would make the choice of not allowing my emotions from the outside interfere with my ability to perform. I was able to form bonds with ladies that have come to be some of my closest friends to this day.

Sophomore year came along and I decided to join the swim team to keep my body conditioned for the upcoming polo season. I was super scared, because I didn't know how to fully do a front flip to the wall. Coaches would see that I would stay behind and try to practice or help the other girls out. When other swimmers would judge my skills and abilities of doing certain tricks, I would use their negative comments to my advantage, as I came to be JV captain of the swim team. This was one of the most rewarding blessings of my life.

I put in the work at all the morning practices, meets, games, and supported my teammates and coaches. Being captain helped me to know what it was to try to be a good leader, a role model that other girls looked up to. That year I began joining many other clubs and had another successful year of polo, since I knew that I wanted to have a well-balanced resume.

As junior year approached, I knew it was time to hit the grind, time for the college process to start. I did all that I could to make sure my college resume was perfect. From National Honor Society to sports to Special Olympics to Chicago Scholars, I filled my resume with every possible extracurricular activity that could get me into a good school. This was the year that my anxiety started to kick in, because I tried to be a perfectionist. It all started with me taking on more AP and college credit classes. The workload got to be a lot. I'd come home at 6:30-7:00 at night from my after-school activities with assignments for each class, volunteer work from clubs, ACT/SAT prep and balancing home life. It was one of the hardest years I ever had to go through just to make sure I was going to get into college. There were nights where I'd stay up 'till 3:00 am doing extra credit homework to make sure I never left any points on the table. I took advantage of what was available for me, and I did the best I could to achieve. There were nights where I was ready to give up and settle for any college, but I remembered what my dad would always tell me growing up: "Go to where the money is." So that's what I did. I applied to many schools and scholarships. I was ready for senior year to come.

LECCIONES AL CORAZÓN

One of my biggest challenges was telling myself that I didn't have to do everything perfect, but to do it with passion and dedication. I found passion in my law classes. I loved the rush of debate and learning about cases around the country and world. For my last two years, I was a part of the mock trial team at my high school, where we would compete against other high schools in the city on various rounds involving cases we studied in class. I got to test the waters to see if I liked the idea of being in a courtroom. From then on, my law teachers would sign me up for law programs around the city, including Loyola Law Academy, for a small course to experience meeting with real lawyers. This opened me up to the idea of becoming a lawyer.

When senior year came around, I decided to run for office in my senior class, winning class Vice President. I did my best to help everyone apply for college, by hosting "senior nights." These events consisted of the senior board helping seniors with their senior checklist, preparing for senior activities, and meeting with seniors and counselors about their risk for not graduating. While trying to juggle everything else going on, I noticed that my stress and anxiety increased. There would be nights that I needed to pull all-nighters, missing out on family events, and not getting to enjoy more of my senior year.

There was one night during senior year that reminded me of my purpose and why I was going through so much stress. That evening, my nana came into my room asking if I was still up, knowing that it was almost 2:00 a.m. I told her that people were counting on me to get things done for senior activities. She told me, *"No vas a poder ayudar a nadie si no te ayudas a ti misma,"* meaning that I can't help others before I help myself first. She always cared about my health, as she tried to give the best advice every time she felt that I needed it.

My last couple months of high school, I was able to continue doing what I loved, which was serving the people and the students. I got to enjoy my hard work and see the smiles of all the students and parents who I helped. One thing that I learned from my high school experience is to be open to new ideas, because you will meet people that will have you seeing life through different eyes.

During the fall of 2019, I was able to continue my studies at University of Illinois in Chicago (UIC), where I'm currently majoring in political science. At UIC I was able to meet new people and join the Latin American Club (LARES). My freshmen year took some getting used to, as more stress got added, but I learned to manage my time more. I look forward to embracing new possibilities to study law abroad. I hope to see myself going to Spain or England to learn about their history, their government, and travel, all in one.

As 2020 began, the idea of studying abroad became a challenge as we experienced a worldwide pandemic that put a pause on certain plans, but certainly isn't stopping them from being accomplished when it's safer for everyone. Through the pandemic, faith was a high factor in my life, as I started to get more involved at my church, where I became a lector and one of the youngest members of Pilsen Generaciones.

While being able to volunteer, I'm able to feel more peace with my nana's passing. Being at church has given me the courage to work on my personal family relationships, allowing me to grow a relationship with my mom at a different stage in my life. Last but not least, give *las fuerzas* to be a part of Young LATINATalks Cicero. Through the process, I got to meet amazing women who helped me in becoming a better public speaker and believer in myself. This leads me to now, being able to share my story in hopes of inspiring you to use the best of your emotions to succeed in life.

THINK YOUNG AND GROW

I encourage you to use your feelings and the power of choice to help you cope with certain situations. We all have more than one feeling that comes to us when we experience something positive or negative. When you feel that your emotions will take the best of you, take a breath and think if it's worth it. You go back to that yes or no question: am I going to let this affect me? I challenge you to try this out. I hope it brings more happiness and clarity to your life.

THIS IS ME

My name is Nicole Denise Barajas. I am a twenty-year-old, young Latina at the University of Illinois Chicago majoring in political science, concentration in pre-law. At this time, I am able to continue to devote my life to community service as a part of the St. Procopius Church in Pilsen, where I volunteer as a lecturer for Sunday service.

Being part of the St. Procopius community, I am embracing my faith as I help Nuevas Gerenaciones, a group of which my father is a member. As my faith grows, this group allows me to grow as a person and reminds me to be grateful for my skills, as they are my blessings from God. Wherever life may take me, I know I will leave my footprint in various hearts and minds. Besides volunteering, I love to cook new recipes from different cultures to expand my food palette and hang out with my friends trying new restaurants.

THE TEN-YEAR PLAN

1. Graduate from law school
2. Establish youth groups in Catholic churches around the nation
3. Take my law school degree to my nanas grave in Mexico

MARISOL NUÑEZ

"Be fearless."

Have you ever felt fearful of doing something that you really wanted to do, and you made a decision that you were just going to do it, in spite of having that fear? Well there I was, standing in the middle of the stage with thousands of people watching, shaking from the fact that I could mess up and make a fool of myself. I was blinded as the spotlight hit my face. My hands were sweaty and my heart was beating faster and faster as if it was going to jump out of my chest. I had only gotten a few hours of sleep that night. Working on a speech the night before its due is no easy task. I had no idea this would be the hardest thing I have ever done, but I stood there with no idea of what would follow—and how much it would change my life.

Let's not get ahead of ourselves. First, let me start from the beginning, and what got me to this exact moment.

MY ROOTS

I grew up less advantaged than most of my peers. I was born in Mexico in a place called Zamora, Michoacán. At only two years of age, my father passed away due to lung cancer. When he passed away, my family was devastated. So much so that my mom brought my older sister and me to the United States in search of a better life, or "the American dream," as they say. My mom requested a visa to go on vacation to Disneyland. However, we never went to Disneyland and arrived at a relative's house instead.

We first came legally in a car with my uncle, who kindly offered to drive us to Chicago, but we overstayed and our passports were no longer valid. My mom had always dreamed of living in Chicago as a teen. I don't remember much, but what I do remember is arriving to my aunt's house, and this weird, fluffy texture was on the ground called snow. I remember seeing a swing set in her backyard and getting so excited for what was about to come. It was a magical day.

Growing up in the United States was hard. We did not know the language, and we had to stay with different family members or in small apartments we could barely afford. I lived in a single-parent household, and a lot of the time my sister and I had to fend for ourselves while our mom was working long ten- to twelve-hour shifts at a factory job. My mom had always been a hard worker, and she had to take me to my babysitter's house at sunrise before work, as early as the age of four, so she could feed her family and make a living.

My relationship with my mom was always up and down. I

felt as if I lived in a toxic household because she was struggling with depression and anxiety, which made her very short tempered. She also has arthritis, and that would always make her very tired. She would take many pills every day, and I honestly don't remember a part in my life when she didn't take any medicine. They were taken to ease the pain she felt throughout her whole body. I could tell she was getting older.

Since she always had to work when I was growing up, I felt as if we never built that strong, emotional connection I truly wanted. I never got the period talk, the boyfriend talk, and to this day, I can't talk about any boy to her. This lack of communication led us to never really having any personal conversations. Even if our relationship was not always the best, I understood why I had to go far in life and *"ponerme las pilas."*

My mom risked it all to come to America so that her daughters could have a better future. She did not go to college and her family did not make a lot of money. This simple fact motivated me so much that it was the first thing I thought about whenever I wanted to give up. Whenever school got hard, I would remember where I came from, and it always pushed me to work harder. There's this quote that I love that says, "When you feel like giving up, remember why you started." I live by this quote, because it makes me remember the reason why I should keep going and not give up, which helped me in many situations.

GAINING CONFIDENCE

When I got to elementary and middle school, it was very

hard for me to have confidence in myself because I struggled with obesity. I weighed 160 pounds at the age of twelve, and I was unhappy. On top of that, I had very crooked teeth, my pronunciation of the English language was horrible, and it was hard for me to learn English. I would always forget how to say certain words in English while translating them in my head. I felt like an outcast. My pronunciation was so bad that I was placed in an ELL (English Language Learners) class for one hour a day, because it was hard for me to have a conversation with someone. I would skip history class and go to a small classroom with a teacher who taught me to read out loud in English to better my pronunciation. Even if these classes were slowly helping me, reading wise, I was the only girl in my class who did not socialize and I stood out, which led to me being bullied for most of my childhood.

I didn't socialize because I was still getting used to not being in a classroom with kids that only spoke Spanish, and I was also still learning how to speak English properly. I was bullied mostly about my weight and lack of communication. I would get called ugly names related to my weight, like, "whale," and some girls would do little things like kick on the back of my seat repetitively to make me mad, knowing I would not have the courage to do something about it.

There was also this one time when I went on a field trip with my classmates to a museum. I was trying my hardest to fit in by talking with a few girls and everything was going well, until we got back to the bus and I was the only one sitting alone. This hurt me very much, and tears rolled down my cheeks on the way back home. I felt like an outsider, like I would never fit in. This bullying changed me because it made me scared of standing out and made me worry about what others would say or think of me.

Once I entered high school, I decided it was time to make a change. I was tired of always feeling insecure and unimportant, feeling worthless and weak. My freshmen year, I joined cross-country and track. I loved this sport because it helped me gain the confidence I needed to make new friends, be more outgoing, and gain leadership skills. It also helped me lose thirty pounds and gain leg muscle, which made me feel strong and physically able to do whatever I pleased. I also got braces, and that helped my pronunciation. I would never smile before, and getting them made me a happier and more confident person.

Throughout my high school journey, I blossomed. I went from being this shy, introverted kid to being a hard worker managing my time between classes, sports, and clubs. I ended up taking six AP classes, joined three sports, and became part of five clubs throughout my high school career, all while maintaining a 4.3 GPA. All the struggles I went through helped me push myself to become a more well-rounded person, and I will forever be thankful of that. I knew how it felt to be at the bottom of the pyramid, and I wanted to have a better future.

As I gained confidence, I started to become more outgoing and began taking risks in high school. I became an officer for the National Honor Society. I became a leader in cross-country. I ran for homecoming princess and won!

By the beginning of senior year, I got the opportunity to participate in a public speaking event to empower Latinas. I was hesitant at first, especially because I was supposed to talk in front of many people and I had never done that. Even if it doesn't seem like it at times, I am still a very shy individual. I hate it because it takes away the enjoyment of unique opportunities and makes me dread doing them.

I gave it a lot of thought and decided I was going to participate, putting aside my lack of confidence and insecurities. That is how I got to that very moment, by taking all the opportunities that crossed my path.

PROCRASTINATION

Before going up on the stage and speaking, I was shaking. I could not believe I was about to share my story with the world. I had barely finished my speech the night before and I knew I was going to make a mistake somewhere throughout my speech. This was my first time doing any type of public speaking, so I made a sticky note to put in my pocket with keywords to help me remember my speech.

Once I started speaking, I could feel people staring at me and saw the camera recording. I felt the pressure, and my face got more red as time went on. It was the most nervous I had ever been in my life. I could not believe I had let myself go through with this. Out of nowhere, my mind went blank. I found myself stuttering and not saying what I had planned. I went ahead and took out the handy notes from my pocket, which helped me to some extent. Being that nervous made it almost impossible to get my point across. Instead of saying, "I want you guys to be fearless," I said, "I want you guys to be fearful," and I did not even notice!

Once I was done speaking, I went back to my seat and my friend texted me mentioning the mistake I had made. I know it was a silly mistake, but I didn't even know how to feel. I wasn't sure if I should feel happy I got to share my message, or embarrassed for messing it all up. One thing I did know was that I was glad it was over. Next time I did a public speech, I'd be sure to be better prepared by not writing my speech last minute and not letting my nervousness get the best of me!

All of my experiences have helped me become the person I am today. Even if I did mess up, I am so happy that I took the opportunity to tell my story, and got to meet amazing people along the way. These amazing Young LATINATalks events led me to meet amazing, inspiring role models such as Minue Yoshida, Angie Ocampo, Jacqueline Camacho, and Gaby Hernandez, who have helped me grow in so many beautiful ways. They helped me get out of my comfort zone and share something personal that the world needed to hear. I experienced talking in front of a large audience for the first time, and the consequences of procrastinating and doing everything last minute.

At the end of the day, I was happy with the result. I still had the opportunity to impact many lives, and that is something I wouldn't change. I am a determined, hard-working young Latina, and I believe that one day, I will accomplish my dreams.

THINK YOUNG AND GROW

Being brave enough to get out of your comfort zone comes with risks. However, don't let that discourage you, and always remember that the long-term benefits of the opportunity are far more beneficial and important. Not only that, but it helps you mature and gain experience as well.

Every risk you don't take is a lost opportunity. I was contemplating being part of the public speaking event, and now I am the co-author of this book at the age of eighteen. You never know what other types of opportunities your decisions could lead you to, so my advice to you is to take every opportunity you come across. Please don't be scared. Getting out of your comfort zone will only help you grow into a more well-rounded person. These risks will also make you happier, due to the amazing people you meet in the process. Be brave and be the person people could look up to and learn from. You got this, *sí puedes!*

THIS IS ME

My name is Marisol Nuñez. I am eighteen years old and a senior at Morton East High School, in Cicero, IL. After high school, I plan on going to Illinois State University for college to study environmental science. I have always felt a natural draw and inclination towards helping the environment, and one day I would like to help fight global warming and climate change.

Once in college, I plan to join many organizations and make the best out of my college experience. Recently, I also got officially accepted for DACA, so I plan to start working right after I graduate high school. I am a very adventurous person and in the future, I hope to travel the world.

THE TEN-YEAR PLAN

1. To get a bachelor's degree and advance in a career that I truly enjoy

2. Get the muscular body I have always aspired to have

3. To live a happy life and make a positive impact in the world

MARIA ALFARO

"It is okay to not be okay sometimes, that is completely normal."

The year 2020 was quite eventful, I am sure we can all agree on that. In some shape or form all of our lives have been impacted by the global pandemic. As 2020 came to an end, I reflected on all the good, the bad, and everything in between; my biggest takeaway was the importance of taking care of oneself. When I say this I mean in every way possible: physically, spiritually, and most importantly, mentally.

Self-care in the simplest of forms can improve your life and change you for the better; not just for yourself, but for those around you. On one of the most anticipated days of the year, I anxiously watched the news. It was election night, and I found myself sitting across from my father's hospital bed, as an air machine helped drain liquid out of his lungs.

Election Day, a day in which my anxiety was already heightened, I accompanied Papi to an imaging test he needed done. After the test was complete, we both walked to our cars; we arrived in separate cars because, Papi being Papi, was going back to work after the appointment. I had driven away, heading home while on Google Meet with my graduate class. Multitasking at its finest. I was doing it safely because my car has Bluetooth.

Fifteen minutes into my drive home, I received a frantic call from my sister. Papi was in the emergency room with fluid in his lungs and in cardiac arrest! I made the sharpest and probably unsafest U-turn of my life, as I rushed to the hospital. I sped down New York Interstate 87 completely confused and at a loss for words. I had watched him get into his car after the appointment; he was fine. What could have happened in those few minutes after I drove away?

Though it was a familiar drive, the emotions I felt at that moment I had never experienced before. I arrived at the emergency room, minutes apart from my sister who was also rushing to the hospital. The staff was anticipating our arrival, as the only words he could mumble while he gasped for air was "call my daughters." As they directed us to where his room was, I watched as my sister ran to hug him, I immediately had to put my poker face on so that I could remain strong for them both. I knew if my younger sister saw me panic, it would make her feel worse. If Papi saw me panic, it would have caused even more stress on his already stressed-out body. Papi was in bad shape. Despite wanting to just break down and cry, I kept it together. I truly thought we were about to lose him.

After a few hours, the doctors were able to stabilize him and he was finally able to tell us what happened. He said that as soon as he saw me drive away, he went to turn on his car, and he immediately lost his breath. He could not breathe. Papi said there was a man standing near his car, so with all the strength in him, he approached the man and told him he couldn't breathe. According to what the emergency room staff told us, the man practically carried Papi into the emergency room, he couldn't recall anything after him telling the man he couldn't breathe. If it wasn't for the angel that God sent to help Papi, he wouldn't be in this world today.

THE REALIZATION

It all hit me the night he was hospitalized, the importance of prioritizing self-care. I spent the night sitting in the chair of his room, ensuring he was receiving the proper care. As I watched him try to get some sleep, all I could think of were all the memories: the happiness, the sorrow and all the special moments shared flashed before my eyes. The thought of losing someone whose words have sustained me was unbearable.

One of the most vivid and impactful memories of Papi was him teaching me how to drive. For as long as I can remember, he wanted me to learn how to drive. Back in El Salvador, he started to drive around the age of fourteen for work, to help his family. Driving is what he knew, so of course it is what he wanted to show me. The first time my dad allowed me to get behind the wheel was when we lived in Florida. I was probably like twelve or thirteen, and he started to teach me how to drive on the dirt roads near where we lived.

As soon as I could get my driver's permit, I did. I was so eager to drive because I knew my dad was so eager to teach me. However, him teaching me how to drive was so much more than driving. Driving big trucks and delivering tires was how he made a living. Therefore, teaching me how to drive was also teaching me independence.

At the time, we lived on a narrow, steep hill, and I was afraid of driving up because I had to get close to the cars that were parked. He'd see me hesitating and he'd say, *"Dale mija, no tenga miedo"* (don't be afraid, keep going). This is something he has constantly repeated to me throughout my life. I remember him telling me this when we'd go horseback riding at Van Cortlandt Park, and I was afraid to get on the pony; when he was teaching me how to ride a bicycle, it was time to take the training wheels off, and I was afraid.

After hearing *"dale mija, no tenga miedo"* so many times throughout my childhood, it has remained embedded in my mind. Until this very day, whenever I feel afraid to do something, I hear his voice in my head and I am able to get myself through whatever it is I'm afraid of. Papi's voice in my head, telling me to not be afraid, helps me get through those things I fear putting myself through. Papi was always easy to talk to and encouraged me to speak with him. Many of his responses were similar to one liners like: *"Póngase las pilas, mija"* (Spanish slang translation: Get yourself together and keep moving). When I did not have the strength to keep on going, it was those words that gave me the push I needed. Hearing this from my father meant for me to find a way to recharge. It meant to continue to make an effort despite the difficulties in life.

If anyone knows how to overcome adversity, it is definitely my dad. Papi immigrated to the United States from El Salvador at the age of twenty-two. He left the known for the unknown, fleeing the ongoing civil war that transpired in the late seventies in El Salvador. Tiny yet powerful, my dad is the strongest and hardest working person I know. My entire life I have watched him work from sun up to sundown to provide for my younger sister and I. He always wanted me to go to school to study and be something in life. He wanted better for me. He didn't want me to have to work as hard as he did, as physically demanding as he did.

My dad is the oldest sibling of his brothers and sisters, as am I. Growing up, a huge part of me felt the need to also work hard. I felt that I needed to show him that all his hard work and sacrifice was not in vain. As soon as I could legally work, I did. At the age of sixteen, I started to work a part-time retail job after school. Shortly after this, I was able to obtain my first office job. Upon graduating high school, I began to work at the office job full-time from nine to five, while attending school full-time from six to nine, twice a week. I did this while also taking online classes. It was work, school, work, school, and more work! Thinking back at that now, I'm not sure how I managed everything, but I did, and I did it well *(or so I thought I did)*. I look back now and realize how much of my time and energy was being put into work and school. I put working hard first because I thought it would be my ticket to success.

Where I come from, the only way to success is by putting in the hard work. However, naturally, there is only so much your mind and body can take before it gives up on you. I learned this the hard way. I started to experience anxiety in different forms. I was so overwhelmed with the hustle and bustle of daily life. However, it was not solely this; as the eldest child of immigrant parents, I also felt the need to be there as much as I could.

There is a unique dynamic between immigrant parents and their first born. I was walking through doors that the generation before me worked so hard to open. I did not want to let them down. My mind was always racing. I had constant fatigue of which I could not shake off and, at times, my heart felt like it was pounding out of my chest. I would try to sit down and complete certain tasks and would start everything on my to-do list, but could never complete one. I was having trouble concentrating, my brain felt so overstimulated by all that I had to do. I felt the only way to calm my racing thoughts was to sleep. This is where the symptoms of my anxiety also led me into depression.

At the time, I had no clue what anxiety or depression was, nonetheless, how to manage it. I was sleeping seven to eight hours and would still wake up tired. I remember going to my primary care doctor and seeking medical guidance, because I thought maybe I had a deficiency causing the excessive tiredness. It got to the point where I would secretly call out of work sick because I could not find the strength to get out of bed. I did not know it at the time, but now realize I was experiencing a deep depression.

I decided to seek cognitive behavioral therapy in hopes of

figuring out what was going on with me. Despite my mind and body giving me signs that I needed to slow down, I kept on going. I had been in therapy for a few months when I experienced my first public panic attack. It was at this point I realized I needed to listen to the signs my body was giving me.

My panic attack happened towards the end of a great night out. A few of my loved ones and I had just driven back to Yonkers from New York City after a Valentine's Day Marc Anthony concert. We decided to grab some late night bites at a regularly visited local restaurant that has live Latin music. All of a sudden, I felt my heart pacing very fast; similar to when I felt anxious, yet different. I noticed my palms were sweaty. I had the chills and felt nauseous. Naturally, I went to the bathroom, thinking maybe the food was simply not agreeing with my stomach. I looked at myself in the mirror and could not recognize the person staring back at me. I took a deep breath, walked back out and tried to carry on with the evening.

As I watched those around me, lost in the music and the moment of enjoyment, I felt overwhelmed. I really had no idea what I was experiencing and, therefore, could not explain what I was feeling to them. It was scary, and though I know I was *not* alone, I *felt* alone because I did not understand what was happening to me. I was able to calm myself down by controlling my breathing.

After several months of having weekly therapy sessions, I was starting to figure out how I could better manage all that I had on my plate. Not only did I learn this, I was also starting to figure out my why. Why did I feel the need to work so hard? To start, I knew that it was what I had seen Papi do my entire life. I also knew that he focused so much on work that he couldn't focus on finding the time to take care of himself.

SURVIVING BUT NOT THRIVING

As I have grown older, so has my curiosity for learning about my roots. I try to engage in conversations with Papi about his childhood in El Salvador and it is like pulling teeth:

Me: "Pa, what was it like growing up in El Salvador?"

Papi: *"Mija, no era fácil, no como se vive acá."* (Daughter, it was not easy, not like how we live here.)

Me: *"Y cómo eran las escuelas?"* (How were the schools?)

Papi: *"Muy diferente de las de acá."* (Very different than the schools here.)

Me: *"Pa, y como eran..."* (Pa, and how were the...)

Papi: *"Mija, mejor hablemos de otra cosa."* (I think it's better if we talk about something else.)

My conversations with Papi about his childhood and El Salvador are short-lived, but I continue to try to ask him and learn more whenever I get the chance. But I get him. As I grow older, I see a lot of myself in my dad, his behaviors, his way of thinking, even his mannerisms. The way we both scratch our heads when we're stressed out. More importantly, I get why he doesn't want to talk about his past; it was filled with trauma from a very young age. He only attended school until the age of about seven. As he tells me, getting to school was hard. It was either you walked miles and miles, or if you were lucky enough, you had a horse to ride.

He started working alongside his father around the age of ten. He helped my grandfather sell fruits, vegetables, and cheese, or any other work he could do to help out the family. Papi also tells me that he was recruited at a young age to help fight against the political turmoil that was transpiring within the Salvadoran government at the time.

Throughout his life, he has dealt with so much and, yet, has remained strong. I know that Papi still battles with the trauma that impacted him as a child. He has never had the opportunity to work through those feelings and understand them. That trauma is probably still stored in his body. The concept of self-care, taking care of our mental health, is such a foreign concept to many immigrants who are barely surviving day to day. It was a foreign concept to me up until a few years ago.

Self-care is absolutely necessary, but not a priority for many within the Latinx community. It is difficult to prioritize yourself when you are constantly working just to survive. Taking the time out to get a massage, to run a bubble bath or to do yoga are all great when you are thriving in life, not merely surviving. To me, this means working nonstop to make ends meet for your family, but not being able to reap the fruits of your labor. Working hard is necessary, but so is prioritizing your mental health.

For some reason, I had trouble turning the on switch off. I desperately needed to rest and take care of me. Through therapy, I was able to learn how to slow things down. I was able to figure out who I was. What I liked, what I didn't like; what made me happy, what didn't. I was discovering who I really was and I loved it. Above all, I was able to unpack the unresolved intergenerational trauma that had been passed down from the generations before me.

What good is the degree, the career, all the success in the world if you are not physically and mentally well? During the pandemic, we all learned a little about how important our overall health is. When the anxiety and depression got the best of me, I was considered a success. I had already earned a bachelor's degree and was halfway done with a master's degree. I had a decent job and I was figuring out my purpose in life. Yet, all of that really meant nothing because I was not happy inside. I had overworked myself to the point of complete exhaustion.

The concept of working all the time, the hustle and bustle, is too over glorified. Titles, salaries and other material items will never fulfill you if you don't take care of yourself. Over-working to the point where we put our work before our own physical health, before our own mental health, is unacceptable.

KNOW BETTER, DO BETTER

All of this is what flashed before my eyes, as I watched Papi sleep in the hospital bed on election night. He had never physically taken care of his body, and he didn't listen to the early signs his body had given him. He didn't know how to; working was all he knew.

I thank God that because of Papi's sacrifices, I have access to therapy, which allowed me to realize sooner than he did in life the absolute need to make sure your own cup is filled before you pour into others. I am grateful that at almost half his age, I have learned to listen to my body, which gives me signs when it's time to rest. Resting allows you to reset and recharge physically and mentally. Our mental health is just as important as our physical health. I have become an advocate for self-care and the impact it has on our mental health.

Mental health within the Latinx community has carried a huge stigma, which is why talking about how we feel is sometimes so hard. My mental health journey has allowed me to finally break through this. It is okay to not be okay sometimes, that is completely normal. The more we talk about this and normalize it, the less we will suffer in silence, which is why being aware is so essential. Being aware of the signs our bodies and minds send us can help us become the best versions of ourselves. Self-awareness allows us to take a step back and really work through our emotions. When we are able to identify what we are feeling, we are then able to better understand how to work through those emotions. Get to know yourself, prioritize yourself, and most importantly, love yourself.

Today, I have a strong head on my shoulders, all thanks to the strength Papi has projected onto me. I continue to hear his voice in my head, *dale mija, no tenga miedo,* whenever I drive in the rain while it's dark. Today, I find myself telling him, *no te preocupes Pa, todo va estar bien,* as I accompany him to the doctors. It's the circle of life. Now that we are both learning about the concept of self-care, he is able to listen to his body and rest when needed, he most certainly deserves to.

THINK YOUNG AND GROW

When you think about self-care, I want you to think about it in the simplest way possible. What small steps will you take in the direction of healing and caring for yourself? Will you take twenty minutes a day to just sit and do nothing? Will you do something again that brought you happiness as a child? I started riding a bicycle again this summer, and it brought me so much joy.

Self-care is not just doing yoga, putting on a face mask, and bubble baths. Self-care is also setting boundaries and knowing the value of your time, it is knowing your worth. It is okay to pause and rest as needed. If the thought of that feels strange to you, I want you to step out of that feeling. Start small. Create a routine. Write out a to-do list. Over time, these small steps will turn into big changes. Now use these small steps to help you step out of that unfamiliar feeling and step into your power: the power of taking care of you. Intentional movements have healing powers on the body. Give it a try.

THIS IS ME

I am a first-generation Salvadoran American from Yonkers, New York. I am the founder of Que Paso Latinx, Inc., a nonprofit organization which sheds light on mental health by educating and empowering the community through healing, conversations, and Latinx culture. I hold a bachelor's in behavioral sciences and a master's in organizational leadership. I am a speaker, leader, and a passionate change-maker in my community.

My dream is to become an international speaker so that I can travel throughout the Caribbean and Latin America sharing my message on mental health awareness. I hope that by sharing my message, I can help normalize society's views on mental health. I also hope that this will help shape how mental health is talked about within our culture, which in turn will better the generations to come.

THE TEN-YEAR PLAN

1. Moving somewhere where I can get daily warmth from the sun, the sun gives me so much life

2. Scaling and expanding my nonprofit, Que Paso Latinx, so that I can make it my full-time work, as it is what fills me with so much joy and purpose

3. Having children that will be able to meet my grandmother, so that they can learn how to pray and how to make homemade tortillas from her, just like I did

STHEFANI ERIKA CAMACHO VASQUEZ

"The key to being happy is knowing you have the power to choose what to accept and what to let go."

As I've gotten older, I've come to realize all the events of my childhood and adolescents had a profound affect on the person I am now. Through all the challenges I've faced, I learned the real meaning of self-love, something that I wish I knew before. If I could send a message to my younger self, it would be the one that I am sharing with you through this story, my story.

My name is Sthefani, and I am a young Latina with Bolivian origins from La Paz, a city that I remember blurrily. Most of my life I have been raised in Spain, since I was four years old. Although I was more connected with my family from Spain and its culture, I always had that Latina side that would characterize me, not only because of my physical appearance or my great skills when dancing salsa, but for knowing that I'm part of that minority that has dreams and doesn't give up until they are reached. As I was writing this, I was reaching two of them: One was getting my bachelor's degree in marketing from Rutgers Business School, and the other one was to write my story in a book.

MY FATHER

My father was a man of many words, knowledgeable, charismatic, patient, loving, and funny. His love made me feel stronger, cared for, and protected. I was so lucky to have him as my father. Unfortunately, like everyone, he had a weakness: alcohol. Since I can remember, he and my mother would have fights and he would disappear for days. Once he was back, he would be very drunk.

I would see my mother crying and distressed countless times, but then everything would be back to "normal" all of a sudden. They would forgive each other and everything would be peaceful as if nothing happened... until the next fight. The whole situation was very confusing when I was in middle school. However, once I started high school, I was used to the cycle, and I already knew what would happen the moment my father would enter the door drunk. It was like an endless replay.

Sometimes I would ignore it and put my headphones on with the loudest music possible, trying to focus on my next exam. It worked most of the time, but I could still feel the door being slammed by my father when leaving the house. It was difficult for me to remain calm and focus on my studies when I didn't know where my father was spending the night, while listening to my mother crying in her room. This always seemed to happen when I had tests or finals the next day. Due to the circumstances, I failed multiple exams, because I would end up crying in silence nonstop in my room until I fell asleep.

Those nights, I felt I couldn't do anything at all. I couldn't stop my father's addiction, and I couldn't stop my mother's tears. I felt incredibly powerless and angry at myself, because I felt I couldn't do anything to help my family. Meanwhile, I was failing another exam. I felt my world was going down. Inside, I was screaming so loud for help, but I didn't know how or who to ask. When I was a teenager, I didn't feel like talking about this with my friends or anyone because I thought nobody would understand my situation, and that people would gossip and judge me. I felt that everyone's life was perfect, and none of my friends had the same problems.

One day, when I was in sophomore year of high school, my father was seen drunk by one of my friends. I felt humiliated, as if I was the one who had done something wrong. I was somewhat mad at my dad, but that was my reality; I could only accept it. I never knew if that was why, but my father decided to stop drinking and joined AA. He was clean for a couple of years. I was very proud and happy, but I had some wounds that couldn't be healed.

When I was in my senior year of high school, getting ready for graduation, I came home to find my father's things were gone. I was confused. I didn't know why he decided to leave and never come back.

That was one of the most traumatic moments of my life, and left me with a big wound. The pain felt very heavy, as if someone had stabbed me in the heart multiple times. I should have been studying for finals, but I couldn't focus. How could I? My father left. After two weeks of crying and feeling like giving up, I realized that I already let his actions affect my life in the past. This time I wanted to fight for myself and not let anything get in the way of what I had worked towards for so long, not even the wound that he caused.

That was the first time I put myself first. The experiences with my family impacted me in such a way that as I grew up, I always prioritized others before myself. However, that blocked me from reaching my goals and loving myself. It was one of the biggest challenges I faced, but I am very proud of myself for not giving up. I had to go to the library from 9:00 a.m. to 9:00 p.m., five days a week for months nonstop. At times, I would sit and reread passages as thoughts of my father invaded my mind, but then I would shake my head, take a deep breath and start reading from the beginning, again and again.

After all my studying, I passed my exams and got in to the university I wanted in Madrid. I will never forget how great I felt, because despite all that was going on in my life, I achieved it. Since that day, I realized that I was capable of that and more. I just had to truly believe in myself. That's when everything changed. That self-realization allowed me to move on and understand that no matter what, I was capable of anything and that I could achieve my goals if I set my mind to it. Unfortunately, there were wounds that were left in me from the experiences with my father that I needed to heal.

At the time, I was in a long-distance relationship with my husband, who was from the United States. We had been together since 2011, and we would fly constantly to see each other every year. We decided to get married, and planned to be reunited after I finished school. He asked me to move with him to the United States a year before my father left, and that was a very difficult decision with all I had on my plate. I didn't want to leave my mother alone. I wasn't ready to move to the United States yet.

After my father left, I reflected on my relationship with my husband. Although we had a strong connection, we had a lot of issues from our past to work through. I knew that I needed a break for a couple of months in order to figure out myself and heal some wounds. I had so much anger and confusion inside of me, despite being strong and wanting to move on with my life, I was still hurt. I knew I couldn't figure out things alone, so I decided to go to a therapist.

I will always be grateful for that choice, because it helped me to understand what was behind all those emotions I was having due to my father and the chaos in my family. However, that was just the beginning of a long journey of healing and self-awareness. After a few months of therapy and lots of thinking, I felt so much better. With a clear mind, I decided to risk my future and everything I had in Spain to be close to the person I loved, my husband.

LOVE AND MENTAL HEALTH

In May of 2016, when I was nineteen years old, I caught a flight with a one-way ticket to the United States. I left behind my family, my friends, and my entire lifestyle. For the first time, I was getting out of my comfort zone and went to start my life from scratch. I still remember how afraid I was, but at the same time feeling so fortunate and happy to be with him.

Time passed by and our bond got stronger because it was him and I facing life together, we went through thick and thin. We worked hard to have our own place and the lifestyle we wanted. I had to adapt to a new language, new culture, new lifestyle, new people, and a new me, but something was not quite okay. I had a lot of responsibilities, such as being a wife, working two jobs, and growing up fast. As I achieved many goals through the years, I couldn't feel good enough. In one day, I could get an honors mention from school or be mentioned as the employee of the month at work and have the biggest smile; then I'd cry later, not knowing why. As the years were passing by, more challenges were added to my relationship with my husband, including communication.

In my first year of college, I joined a club called Active Minds, a club that supports mental health awareness and education for students. Later on, I became the president of that club. That was the door that enlightened me to know the importance of my mental health—and that I needed help. Although I thought I was doing okay managing school, my relationships, and work, I was not. People say that the first step is to admit it, but that's easier said than done. Nevertheless, I didn't want to avoid what was behind my emotions, because they weren't letting me live my life to the fullest. They were getting heavier as I was trying to reach my goals. So, I started counseling again and learned something crucial. My father's abandonment caused me to think that I was never good enough, and that's why I always had to do more than I could. For example, I would be involved in many activities in school, I would get straight A's, and I would work so hard to be recognized at my job. I cared so much what people would think of me because my past was haunting me. I felt like I needed to be perfect in order to be included because when my father left, I felt rejected. I was looking for other people's approval, instead of finding approval from myself. All this led me to perfectionism and anxiety.

As I started working on my mental health, I began to open my eyes to many more things I was not aware of; one of which was related to my husband. For many years after my father left, I was more attached to him. No matter how many fights or hurtful words would cross between us, I couldn't imagine my life without him. However, we both had a challenging past and didn't know how much it would affect our relationship before we got married. As with many couples, we didn't realize these issues because we were so much in love, but that love was fading away.

One day in 2019, I had enough. I loved my husband with all my heart, but I realized that I didn't deserve to feel the way I was feeling, and neither did he. For all the experiences we shared together and how much he meant to me, it was not fair to either of us. We did all that we could to make our relationship work, but there were things we couldn't change for each other because that's how we truly were. Although people can change, it was not fair to demand that of each other, because then that wouldn't be love.

That same year, I realized how much I was emotionally dependent on him and how afraid I was to start my own path. As Al-Anon (support groups for family members of an alcoholic) literature says: "Detachment is neither kind nor unkind. It does not imply judgment or condemnation of the person or situation from which we are detaching. It is simply a means that allows us to separate ourselves from the adverse effects that another person's alcoholism can have upon our lives." Although my husband was not a drinker, as a child of an alcoholic I had a hard time with detachment. I had to reprogram myself and I felt very lost, not knowing who I was anymore. Everything was so confusing, but the beautiful thing about life is that endings are just new beginnings. The key to being happy is knowing you have the power to choose what to accept and what to let go.

SELF-LOVE AND GETTING OUT OF MY COMFORT ZONE

In December of 2019, I decided to go visit my mother in Spain and spend Christmas with her and my brother. During my time there, I created a list of all my fears and all the things that I wanted to do to help me get out of my comfort zone. I had never done anything like that before.

One of the things to do on my list consisted of dancing with my mother to a Bee Gees' song in the middle of the city in Madrid and video record it. You may think it's silly, but that moment meant so much to me. I have always been shy and cared what people thought. However, that day I enjoyed having fun with my mother and not caring at all about the people looking at us. A twenty-three-year-old daughter dancing with her mother in the middle of Madrid… that was priceless.

That was the trigger I needed. Since then, I have been spending more time with myself and exploring the city alone. This was very challenging for me, but I knew that I had to practice more detachment and more me-time. Therefore, I would take my backpack and would go to museums, restaurants, and many other places alone. I video blogged in some places and started narrating my stories in public. Some people would look at me strangely, but I was having a blast!

After I visited my family in Spain, I returned to the United States as a new person. I wanted to continue the self-development and self-love journey I had already begun. So, in 2020, I started a journal. I can't believe how much I underestimated the power of writing, because it helped to clear out my mind, be present, and manifest my life. I found this to be the key to comprehending my deepest thoughts and it allowed me to reconnect with myself.

After meditating or working out, I still write in it. I find it very helpful to relieve my mind from overthinking. Journaling was another resource I used to heal from my past. What I once wrote when crying, I now read with a humble smile because it reminds me of all that I have gone through, and it doesn't hurt like before. Another important thing I learned when journaling

TODAY'S INSPIRED *Young* LATINA VOLUME III

was to write about the things I was grateful for. That allowed me to appreciate more of my life, including everyone around me and the little things in life such being able to wake up one more day. Trying new things every week helped me to gain confidence and love myself as I never did before.

Some people ask me if I regret getting married when I was very young, and my answer is no. The choice I made at that moment was the best choice for me, because I genuinely loved him. I decided to take the risk, and I will always be grateful that I did. I will always keep the best memories we made together with me, and I will always wish him the best for his life. In the end, the experiences that I lived were the ones that made me wiser and appreciate my life more.

Sometimes, it's difficult to accept that we have things to solve emotionally. We don't feel prepared to face it, but I don't think we will ever be completely ready for something like that. Since my father left until now, I have been using therapy, journaling, and physical activity as my main pillars to help myself understand what's under all these feelings and thoughts. I allowed myself to unwrap many memories from my past that were in my subconscious and affect my present, and start healing them one by one.

I don't know where my father is now, but wherever he is, I hope he is okay. If he ever reads this, I would like him to know that I forgive him. Most important, in this challenging journey, I learned to forgive myself for being so hard on myself. Although this journey continues, I know that I broke free from the things that weren't letting me move on completely and found true peace in my life; that's worth all the hard work.

Since I was a little girl, I wanted to help my family and the people around me, because I was wounded and I didn't want others to feel that way. Eventually, I understood that to help others, first, you have to help yourself. I always use the example of the oxygen mask rule that flight attendants tell you on airplanes: "Please place the mask over your mouth and nose before assisting others." For the longest time, I thought it was selfish to put on my own mask first. I thought that taking care of myself first was selfish. After all my life experiences, I finally understood that taking care of yourself is not selfish; it's essential.

THINK YOUNG AND GROW

Everything begins in your mind. If you want to change, you have to start with your thoughts. You have to be willing to face that overwhelming place where thoughts and feelings are together. You have to be willing to go deep down through all the layers and find the root of the problem. Don't let time pass by, don't think that time will heal it by itself. You have to do your part; you have to conquer your fears and meet your pain halfway to let them go.

Remember that your choices become your actions, and your actions become your habits. Therefore, use any resource you can. Take the time and space you need. Try new things, and reconnect with yourself; in the end, you have only one life to reach all your dreams. Don't let the past haunt you or block you from reaching them. Start healing those wounds and fall in love with yourself, because you are unique and worth it. You are good enough.

THIS IS ME

My name is Sthefani Erika Camacho Vasquez. I am currently a senior at Rutgers University, majoring in marketing with a supply chain concentration.

My dream for the future is to create an organization or business that helps people have a better life and achieve their goals. I want to keep using my life experiences to motivate others to get out of their comfort zones.

THE TEN-YEAR PLAN

1. Become a content creator that helps others achieve their goals by creating healthy habits
2. Achieve a life with financial stability and independence
3. Taking my mother with me to travel the world and make more memories together

CIPOTA CACHIMBONA: STRENGTH IN VULNERABILITY

SANDRA GONZÁLEZ

"Accept your vulnerabilities and turn them into your greatest strengths."

In Salvadoran diasporic communities, a cipota cachimbona is a strong and resilient woman, and that is who I am. As a minority within a minority, a Central American person living in an area where the Latinx community is primarily of Mexican descent, I have found that being a cipota cachimbona is more than being a strong woman. I have embodied this through the professional, academic, and emotional hurdles I have faced, and continue to overcome with the help of my chosen family. It has allowed me to accept my vulnerabilities and not let them define my way of persisting. In the end, my mental health struggles have taught me that I can be a cipota cachimbona who embraces the moments in which I question myself because, through it all, I am who I am because of the strength in my vulnerability.

There are very few details I know about my parents' migration experience, along with their childhood stories, as a result of the generational trauma caused by a civil war that was fueled by the U.S. intervening politically in Central America throughout the seventies into the early nineties. I do know that in 1992 my parents migrated to the United States while my mom was three months pregnant with me, with the hope of escaping a war-torn country, one that would have otherwise not fostered opportunities for their children to break the cycle of poverty they experienced. My mom has said they made their way through México and when she and my dad got to the border, they separated and planned to meet in Chicago, Illinois. They sought asylum at a time when it was not as challenging for INS (Immigration and Naturalization Service) to admit migrants on the basis of ongoing political turmoil in a person's country of origin.

After arriving in Chicago, my parents stayed with my dad's family until they were able to save up enough money to get a home of their own. My dad was always someone who worked diligently to be successful and, while they had to start over in the United States, he was the only one out of fifteen siblings to graduate with a university degree in business administration and accounting from la Universidad Salvadoreña de Alberto Masferrer. He wanted to go into chemical engineering, but the cost of tuition forced him to change his career that eventually led him to work for the Salvadoran government. Although his degree did not translate immediately to a high-paying position in the

U.S., it did not deter him from working and taking accounting and real-estate courses that resulted in him becoming a certified real estate broker. His passion for learning was something that was ingrained in me from a young age.

However, growing up in a home where mental health was not acknowledged, let alone receiving help to understand the constant feeling of not being good enough, was something that took a while for me to discover. In general, Latino immigrant families experience mental health as a taboo, not to be discussed. Receiving medical attention for it was either discouraged or hidden from family for fear of embarrassment. As a result, it wasn't until college when I was an adult on my own that I learned that I had been living with depression and anxiety as far back as middle school. I was then diagnosed with attention deficit disorder in the fourth semester of my doctoral program, in the middle of a worldwide pandemic. My mental illnesses, while I am still learning to navigate and have my family understand how they impact my day to day, are the vulnerabilities that I believe to also be some of my greatest strengths.

VULNERABILITY AS A WEAKNESS

Before I started my freshman year of college, I originally wanted to be an orchestra director. By my senior year in high school, I had a love for fine arts. I participated in choir, band, and orchestra. I wanted to teach high schoolers. I was influenced by my orchestra director who not only helped me grow in my ability to play viola, but also taught me what it meant to care for students.

My dad's reaction to my decision was nothing but crushing to my confidence. He felt that I would not be able to find a job and boiled it down to me not being strong in science and math. The easy way out as he said. To add to that he felt that I should have probably considered becoming a lawyer. All I wanted was to teach high school orchestra.

When I went to audition for the school of music, I did not make the cut, which gave my dad more fuel to bully me. I entered a state of sadness and lacked joy, so much so that I grew disinterested in my music classes. I went through the motions the remainder of my senior year of high school, and I still had no idea that I was experiencing depression or even withdrawing from the things that used to be emotional outlets.

I was indifferent about going away to college, due to not getting into music school to become a music teacher. My dad had continued to make fun of me for my plans not coming to fruition, and I spent the summer leading up to leaving for college in a depression, but I had learned to mask it well in front of others. Part of why I left for Northern Illinois University (NIU) was because I was still set on becoming a high school teacher and they are known for their teaching college. But I also knew that if I went to a college close to home, like my dad would have liked, my mental health would have been further jeopardized. I did not know it at that time, but I would later be diagnosed with major depressive disorder and generalized anxiety.

My first semester at NIU was challenging. I spent much of the first semester consumed with figuring out whether I wanted to try to get into music school again or pursue a different education field. Much of what I thought I knew about college went out the window as I was no longer being guided by teachers and I didn't have the motivation I thought I had, that stemmed from the disappointment in myself. I failed two classes and was placed on academic probation with a GPA of 1.92.

When I came back for the spring semester after a winter break of my dad questioning my choice to go to NIU, I declared myself a Spanish education major. I was told that because I knew the language, I was taking the easy way out. My response to him: "Not everyone can teach." I would prove him wrong.

I gradually got my GPA up, finding spaces on campus, like the Latino Center, that allowed me to grow at NIU. Even though I was determined to be successful, the voices in my head that would question my every move would eventually get the better of me. Spring semester of my sophomore year, I was sitting in my dorm room following an incident where someone on my floor criticized me for not being social enough and not having many friends. Although it seemed like nothing, it triggered the trauma I faced from my dad, which led to a four-day weekend of crying myself to sleep, not eating, and feeling alone.

My floor leader found it strange that he had not seen me in a few days and my boyfriend, who was concerned for my well-being, convinced me to visit the health center psychiatrist. I was diagnosed with depression and anxiety. I went back to my room and felt as though the world was crumbling around me. Mental illness was a taboo in my house and continues to be taboo among many older Latinx generations. I decided to take medication and go to group therapy. I was encouraged by my friends and my boyfriend to take care of myself after learning about their experiences with mental health care.

Going to therapy at that time was new. I felt ashamed for my vulnerabilities being visible in my life. It would be years until I would tell my mom about my mental health struggles and, until then, I was adamant about hiding what I thought was a weakness. It was hard to come to terms with having multiple mental illnesses, which is actually common as I would eventually learn. Trying to tell my family that this was something that was affecting me was challenging, considering it was a subject we never discussed.

Finding the right therapist was not an easy feat. I opted for group therapy because I thought it would be an easy fix with the campus counseling center, in addition to using NIU's health services to have medication prescribed by a psychiatrist. Listening to other students' struggles made me feel for a moment that I was not alone, and it was through the recommendation of my residence hall floor leader that I even sought out that style of therapy. As I told my closest friends about therapy, they opened up and told me about their experiences with different medications, which led me to being put on my first antidepressants. I spent a full semester in therapy coupled with my medication, and I felt that I was in a good place to not continue with therapy after the semester was over, as I felt my medication was working.

By my senior year of undergrad, I was presented with

multiple opportunities. I joined the honors program, was an undergraduate researcher for the Center for Latino Studies, received scholarships and finished my education licensure requirements. By the time graduation rolled around, my GPA was 3.7, and I was one of three students recognized by the NIU president during our commencement for being an exemplary student. In spite of these accomplishments, the relationship between my dad and I remained rocky. My college graduation made him proud, but not the path I took to get there. Needless to say, graduation was a bittersweet moment for me.

I decided not to move back home, and instead I moved into my friend's home to be closer to my first teaching job as a Spanish for Native Speakers teacher. With the support of my friend and my fiancé, I was able to find my passion for Latinx students and be involved in my community in Aurora. It was through my three years of teaching there that I became a community organizer and became part of creating the Aurora Rapid Response Team, a nonprofit that fights with and for immigrant families. However, my mental health issues would once again take center stage.

OWNING MY VULNERABILITIES

I graduated from NIU in the spring and was stoked to start my first teaching position. I began teaching high school Spanish for native speakers and was happy to contribute some of my own cultural knowledge to the curriculum as someone from a Latino community that is not often represented in areas that are largely of Mexican descent. It was an opportunity for me to teach my students more about other Latin American cultures on top of further exploring their own identities. As I got more involved in my school's community, the more I saw a need to advocate for students whose own immigration status or their family member's status impacted their schooling experience, due to a rise in anti-immigrant rhetoric around the U.S. and me being from a mixed status family, a family where at least one person is not a U.S. citizen.

As I started asking about more ways in which my district was supporting undocumented students and students from mixed status families, the greater attention I was receiving around my teaching style, professionalism, and regard for expectations versus reality. After three years, I was not asked to return to my teaching position. This greatly affected my mental health. The culmination of teaching full-time and questioning the system that was meant to support students did have its consequences.

My advocating for students from mixed-status families was not appreciated in the last year of my first teaching position, and therefore resulted in administrators challenging the decisions I would make both in and out of the classroom. It made me question the decisions I made, and in effect grew my imposter syndrome, which is when people of color in particular question their capabilities in spaces that were designed to keep us out. I eventually found another teaching position not far from my first district, where I taught Spanish for native speakers for a year because I was filling in for someone on maternity leave. I carried my advocacy for students and mixed-status families into that district. Similar to my previous district, many students affected by this issue were not being supported in the ways they needed to be.

Throughout that time, my mental health concerns grew to the forefront of much of my life, and went unaddressed until I began seeing a Latina therapist that understood my lived experiences without needing to probe too much into my childhood trauma. What she addressed was my imposter syndrome, the voice in my head that came and went. I felt like I was getting smaller and smaller as I chipped away at the wall of emotions.

When 2018 came, I was questioning my career choice, my worldview, and letting my depression and anxiety fester. In May 2019, I graduated with my master's in diversity and equity in education from the University of Illinois Urbana-Champaign and two weeks later, started my doctoral program at Illinois State University. Never did I think that I would be pursuing a Ph.D., but I decided to do so because I felt that the program would allow me to find the thing, the knowledge, to continue advocating for students outside of the realm of teaching.

I moved on to another district for the 2019-2020 school year, where I taught AP Spanish to native speakers for a semester. After five years of teaching, I left my teaching career to address my mental illness. My community organizing and view of K-12 education taught me that I loved being with students, but not as a teacher. I experienced a depressive episode, even with seeing my therapist regularly, where I could not get myself out of bed for four days. I knew that I needed to move on to find myself and I resigned. My plan was to go into higher education and little did I know that a pandemic would take over in March 2020.

My unresolved mental health issues were exacerbated after resigning, to the point that in March 2020, I was hospitalized for four days for suicidal thoughts. After a build-up of family disagreements that culminated with the thought of hurting myself, I spoke with my therapist, who advised me to admit myself. The same night I had my therapy session, I packed my bag, told my husband to drive me to the hospital, and had to then communicate through him to my professors that I would need extensions on my homework. That weekend was the same weekend that the first of the COVID shelter-in-place mandates took effect, which meant I was not allowed any visitors.

I spent four days in the hospital, learning more about why I admitted myself, having psychiatrists change up my medication, and then create a plan with the hospital therapist for out-patient treatment. The first week of April 2020, I started my out-patient treatment, which consisted of several mindfulness group sessions, one-on-one with the facility's therapist, while also checking in with their psychiatrist over how I was reacting to the new medications. Unfortunately, I went for three days before having to check myself out as a result of the growing threat of COVID-19. In lieu of going every day for treatment, I came up with a plan with my regular therapist and psychiatrist to check in with them remotely as often as their schedules allowed in a given week to make up for not being in the out-patient program.

The pandemic exposed another issue that had been creeping up in my doctoral studies. In my fourth semester for my Ph.D. program, July 2020, I was diagnosed with ADHD by my psychiatrist after experiencing brain fog, the inability to focus, for a year during the program. It made it impossible to focus on reading or writing for more than 10 minutes and impacted my short-term memory. Something as simple as where I put my keys would be hard to decipher and still is now. We are still playing around with my ADHD medications, given I was already on antidepressants, but I am always making sure to couple these with non-medicinal methods, like study and time management strategies, to alleviate some of the challenges I deal with when working on projects.

It was these experiences that finally sparked the need for me to make my vulnerabilities my strengths and learn to accept that it is okay to not be okay. During 2020, I spent time reflecting on my vulnerabilities and taking ownership of my own emotions in relation to how I communicate my mental health struggles to those closest to me in my family—and to an extent professionally. Where I once felt consumed by the voices in my head as a means to diminish my successes on the basis of the emotional turmoil my dad would perpetuate, I have since shared my experiences with people like my mom and others that have become a part of my chosen family to alleviate the burden I carried on my own for the longest time.

REFRAMING MY VULNERABILITIES

Working with my therapist on ways to acknowledge my mental illnesses and shaping them into positives has helped me see how to navigate them in a way that is not a deficit. Knowing what my reactions are to adverse emotions with my depression and anxiety, while also understanding how these feed my ADHD and vice versa, has been no easy task. I understand that there are episodes where my depression will get the better of me, like not having the motivation to get out of bed, but I know that even if I just wash up to get the day started, it could potentially help me to get one thing out of the day. I know that if my focus is only for so long, I use a timer to take breaks in between reading for school or writing, to make tackling homework easier. These may sound like simple solutions, but sometimes it does take a lot to do these!

I am still reframing my vulnerabilities, my major depressive disorder, generalized anxiety, and ADHD, into experiences that have allowed me to learn and see myself as a cipota cachimbona. I feel it is important to understand this feeling because I want people to know that while people may seem a certain way on the outside, you never know what hurdles they may be going through on their own to be that person you see in front of you. Although the voices in my head remain, I lean more on my husband to talk through what I am feeling in that present moment. I see my struggles as even more of a mission to show people that here is a young woman, a daughter of immigrants, the first in her family to pursue a doctoral degree, who continues to find strength in vulnerability.

I want younger Latinas, *las cipotas*, to know that we each have distinct mental health journeys and where someone may think of having a mental illness as a weakness, I say to them that being vulnerable has opened my eyes to living beyond what society sees as my limitation. There is strength in my vulnerability, and I continue to grow into this reframing of my journey in order to strengthen my advocacy and foster healthy relationships with those I love.

THINK YOUNG AND GROW

Being vulnerable continues to be a challenge during a time where we are asking each other to unlearn to learn for our communities and for our own growth. My questions for you are: What makes you feel like an imposter? How are you addressing those emotions? I believe these to be important questions, because it allows us to think about how we are healing, how we are processing, and how we react in situations that challenge our mental health. We cannot control how others affect our mental well-being. What we can do is allow ourselves a moment to reflect on our own terms, to continue on the path of turning our vulnerabilities into our greatest strengths.

THIS IS ME

I'm Sandra González. I am the oldest daughter of Salvadoran migrants. I'm a doctoral student (Ph. D.) at Illinois State University studying educational administration and foundations and am the first in my family to complete a university degree in the United States. I ran for office for the first time to be a Waubonsee Community College trustee for the April 2021 local elections and serve as the executive director of an immigration advocacy organization, The Aurora Rapid Response Team. I aspire to become a professor of Central American studies, a director of a university cultural center, or a director of programs that are directed at the success of students who are the first in their families to go to college.

THE TEN-YEAR PLAN

1. Graduate with my Ph.D. in educational administration and foundations by May 2024

2. Take my husband to El Salvador for the first time ever

3. Work in a university as a professor or director and continue to advocate for justice in education

GROWING UP

YARITZA VALLEJO

"I reached a point in life where things started to make sense."

My name is Yaritza Vallejo and I was born and raised in Des Plaines, Illinois. I was raised in a traditional Mexican household, influenced by typical Hispanic gender roles. My mother's primary responsibility was to maintain a clean home and to make sure there was always warm food to be served. While my dad's first and only responsibility was to provide for his family financially. I believe that these traditional gender roles made it difficult for me to know exactly what I wanted and how to get there, because I was accustomed to seeing my mother only doing certain things. For a time, I thought that women were limited in what they could do, and therefore I would have limited options when it came to be choosing a career path. Coming from a Hispanic household doesn't just mean you speak Spanish, it comes with its own set of cultural norms and family beliefs.

When it came to academics, like many other parents, mine

235

wanted me to excel. That desire for my success quickly became an expectation that would eventually lead to pressure throughout my education. I felt like my parents expected me to always know what I wanted and how I would get there. Nonetheless, the bar was set high for me, and there was very little to no room for excuses.

BLINK OF AN EYE

I was finishing up sixth grade when my parents began talking about moving to Mexico. The 2008-09 recession was hurting my dad's job. He worked in construction and went months without working. He was constantly stressed and trying to find jobs he could pick up, but with no luck. There was nothing I could say or do as a twelve-year-old. They decided to move us to Jalisco, Mexico.

I dreaded the day that we were set to leave. I felt devastated that I had to leave my school without saying a word to my friends, since everything was very sudden. I complained and cried the whole way. I felt left out; I felt nobody wanted to hear what I had to say. Wasn't I part of the family? I felt nobody cared where I was in life and like I wasn't taken into consideration. I had always tried to live up to my parents' standards, and I felt it was for nothing.

Growing up they expected me to be the perfect child, bring home the best grades, and I felt that I accomplished it, but it seemed I was being punished for it instead of being rewarded. I took this personally, because I felt nobody had asked me if I was okay with moving nor asked how I felt. Looking back, I understand why they made the decisions they did. As a sixth grader, I did not realize everything that went into play when deciding that we were moving. At that moment, I forgot my parents were not only my parents, but humans too.

Moving to a new place is hard. Anyone who has experienced it knows that it feels like you're starting all over again, and it's daunting. I was going through middle school and part of high school with fear of failure. I didn't feel like I fit in and couldn't be honest with my parents regarding how I felt because I believed they would think it was me being childish.

There was always something holding me back, but that was just myself. I think moving to Mexico grew my fear of failure because I felt I had to play catch up. The education system is very different, and the primary language spoken in Mexico is Spanish. At the time, my Spanish was not at its best, and I was very focused on improving my reading and writing skills.

While I felt like I was living in fear, I was also gaining a lot of knowledge and exposure. I became very fluent in Spanish and developed some of my closest friendships, that wouldn't have happened if I hadn't moved to Mexico. By living in Mexico, I learned about the beautiful culture and traditions they have, and overall became a more well-rounded person.

After four years, my parents decided to move back to Des Plaines, IL. My dad received a job offer and really wanted my brother and me to be return to school in the United States. He strongly believed we would have more opportunities and access to better schools.

I was excited, but terrified to go back. I was sixteen and had no idea what I was doing with my life. I felt like I lost four years of my life and my parents didn't understand how I felt. My parents thought I was making a big deal out of the situation and dismissed my feelings.

Moving back to United States presented a challenge for me. I always claimed I felt lost because I was in Mexico, but what could I blame now? It seemed to be that I could never really nail down what I wanted. I had thought I wanted to move back to Illinois. It took me time to learn to appreciate moving to Mexico. While I was living in Mexico I questioned why we moved. I felt there weren't many opportunities for me and that I wouldn't get anywhere in life. Living in the United States represented endless opportunities. Moving to Mexico represented a hardship I had to overcome. It was an emotional time, and ultimately shaped the person I am today.

While I was excited to be back and see my old friends, I was also worried that I wouldn't fit in anymore. During my first couple of weeks back in school, I felt very nervous and shy. I wasn't sure if I was speaking proper English or if people looked at me funny since I had been gone for four years. My mind was all over the place, and I was having a hard time concentrating in class.

As time went on, I slowly began to feel more comfortable and started getting out of my comfort zone by participating in class and joining school organizations. I came to realize that moving to Mexico showed me how to be more understanding and appreciative of opportunities. I went from feeling like I had no opportunities to being able to attend college and all the opportunities that could come with that.

I graduated high school in 2016 and had absolutely no clue what I was going to do moving forward. I had big dreams. I wanted to have a successful career, be financially stable, and travel around the world. I wanted to show younger girls that we can accomplish anything that we set our mind to, no matter how big or small that goal was. Even though I knew what I wanted my life to look like, I had no idea how to get there.

It's unsettling to realize that you have big aspirations but don't know where to begin. I felt pressure, and even anxiety at times, because I was trying to control my emotions. I did not want to break down or feel the sadness that I knew was coming. There were thousands of thoughts in my head and sometimes I just felt like I couldn't take it anymore. I felt discouraged and overwhelmed. I didn't know what I was doing and figuring it out as I went. Once again, I felt lost in life and this time it wasn't because I moved. I felt as if I had so many questions and no answers to them as time went on.

I began listening to podcasts about motivation and talking to different people about their experiences. I paid attention to the way they were able to overcome obstacles and the attitude they had. I came to learn that it's okay to not know what you're doing out of high school, and that it doesn't mean you won't be successful in life. There's an expectation from society of having your life figured out when you graduate high school, but it's rare

239

that you do. Not only are recent graduates trying to figure out what they want to do, but they're dealing with relationships, family, addictions, and so many other things we may not know about that are going on in their life.

THE TRANSITION

There's a misconception of what success looks like out of high school. Many consider success to look like attending a four-year institution with a high price tag attached, or attending an Ivy League school with some of the brightest people in the world. For a long time, I fell into this fallacy. I attended community college after high school and felt frustrated with myself for not attending a four-year institution, like I originally planned, due to my ACT score not being high enough to earn a scholarship. I blamed the move to Mexico for where I was attending school, and took no responsibility for my lack of effort when studying. I thought that moving to Mexico put me behind in my studies, since the curriculum is slightly different, and my English reading and writing skills were not the best after living in Mexico for four years.

I was working and attending school full-time. My energy was focused on work because I felt I was good at it and I found a sense of belonging with it. I was working at a dental office and for a moment, thought I found my passion. I felt I was learning at a rapid pace and enjoyed working with my team. While I was thriving at work, I was lacking in school. I would go to class and leave. The only effort I was putting in was attending class. I found myself demotivated and doing just enough to get by academically. I felt very alone on this journey, because my parents were very hands off during this time. They gave me a lot of freedom to make my own decisions, but I interpreted that as a lack of interest.

During my second year of community college, I met Franklin Ortega. He was an advisor for ANDALE, a Latinx organization at the community college I attended. I met him by accident. I was walking with a friend to class and she stopped to see him and introduced us. He was intrigued by my persona and began asking lots of questions. He was very welcoming and I appreciated the interest. I eventually saw him again and he insisted on scheduling an advising appointment with him. Again, he asked a lot of questions about my interests and was genuinely excited to get to know me. I could not comprehend why; I felt like I was the least impressive person in the school. He asked me to join ANDALE and insisted I go to one of their weekly meetings. I was hesitant to go, because I felt that it wouldn't change anything about me, but I decided to attend.

I walked into the meeting and instantly saw the enthusiasm in the other students' faces. I overheard a few conversations regarding their current internships and the plans they had upon completion of school. I felt overwhelmed and immediately left. I was scared and intimidated, seeing all these students who knew what they were doing, but I had no clue.

I didn't understand what was going on with me. One of my goals was to earn a degree and make my parents proud, but I was reluctant. I constantly asked myself why I wasn't motivated to put in the work and found no clear answer.

Franklin kept reaching out and sending me resources. For some reason I felt I could trust him, he seemed to genuinely care about how I felt and my success. We had another advising appointment and he asked, "What do you really want in life? What gets you up in the morning?"

I instantly felt my face get red and tears rolled down my face. I looked down and whispered quietly, "I don't know."

He looked at me, gave me a tissue box, and said, "That's okay, it doesn't mean we can't figure it out." For the first time, I felt a sense of hope for my future. We began talking more about what I liked and disliked. I was interested in becoming a dentist or an attorney. These two careers were my starting point for figuring out what I wanted to do.

Before I left his office, he told me, "I believe in you, you just have to believe in yourself."

I had never heard those words being said to me, not even by my parents. I left the office feeling excited. I never imagined that somebody I had just met out of the blue would change my mindset forever. I quickly began analyzing my life, and knew the end of two years at community college approached. I was not looking forward to staying there because I felt too comfortable and did not feel challenged. I knew it was the smart thing to do, but I was just not invested. I had a full-time job where I was extremely comfortable, but I was very aware that the room for growth was limited. I enjoyed my job at the dental office, and I think a big reason for this was because I knew I was good at it. This provided validation and a sense of security.

STARTING OVER

The more I thought about my future, the more I realized what I wanted it to look like. I knew I needed to attend a university. I wasn't motivated at my community college and I felt a traditional university setting would get me to the places I needed to go a lot sooner. One afternoon, I began looking up universities in Chicago and applied to several of them.

A few weeks later, I got an acceptance from DePaul University and would start school within three months. I was excited to be accepted, but also terrified because I knew this would take me out of my comfort zone. Part of me felt validated in my abilities and another part felt I ran the risk of not being smart enough. I looked at the price tag and knew there was no feasible way of paying out of pocket. I began looking into loans and applied. I had built my credit for a couple years and luckily my loan applications were accepted.

I asked my parents to come with me to a college visit. They did, but didn't really say much. They didn't understand what was going on; they just saw it as another school, an expensive school. My parents did not attend college, and therefore it limited how involved they were in the process. I tried explaining how things worked, but everything was very new to them.

As a first-generation college student, there were a lot challenges and things I had to learn on my own. I had to figure out a lot on the spot, whether it was FAFSA, making a resume, or learning to network with professionals. I felt alone in the process, but I understood why.

I didn't tell Franklin I was transferring until after I made the decision. I knew he would say it wasn't smart to transfer yet. I could still complete credits at community college to transfer to a four-year institution and save money.

I was afraid to fail, but I knew that if I stayed, I would remain too comfortable. I signed my acceptance to DePaul and quit my job. I felt like I was too comfortable with my job, and that it was holding me back from advancing my education. That was one of the hardest moments I'd faced. I had just quit everything that made me comfortable. I quit the only source of income I had and what I knew.

My commute to DePaul consisted of at least two and a half hours a day on the CTA, five days a week. I left my house at 6:00 a.m. and wasn't back home until around 10:00 p.m. every day. By the time I was home, the only thing I wanted to do was sleep until it was time to get up again. I was exhausted. Not only was I physically active all day, but I was constantly doing homework, studying, and trying to figure out if I should even stay with my declared major.

Initially, I went in with a biology major because I wanted to be a dentist. However, I disliked my biology courses. I soon realized that biology was not going to work for me. It was mentally draining to go through studying and homework, but it became an emotional drain when I realized I was not in the right major. I was afraid of changing majors, because I thought that was a sign that I still didn't know what to do with my life. I was already in debt and felt like I had to finish to pay back my loans as soon as possible.

The following quarter I decided to switch my major to business. I really enjoyed what I was learning about economics. It dealt with problem-solving analytical skills, but also related to human behavior. Everyone in my class was sharp and had an impressive resume. I didn't even have one!

I came home one night feeling discouraged and began doubting myself. All the students at DePaul were unbelievably smart and I didn't feel I was cut out for it. My mom reminded me that I could accomplish anything I wanted, and that it was really up to me and my own determination. I had no job and didn't have anything to fall back on. I went to sleep and went back to school.

I started looking into internships and clubs at DePaul. Eventually I found one that sparked my interest: Association of Latino Professionals for America (ALPFA), a Latinx business club. I went to the first meeting and they needed a secretary on board, and I offered to do it. I've never been involved in any club, but I realized this was the opportunity I needed to get involved. They accepted me just the way I was and pushed me to do better. I made friends who had the same goals and similar experiences, such as earning a degree and empowering those around them. I finally had a group of people I could relate to.

I felt motivated to do well in school and go after my goals. Meeting students that I could relate to really changed my perspective and pushed me to want to do better. I began surrounding myself with people who were ambitious and were working toward earning a bachelor's degree. I didn't feel alone anymore. I started enjoying attending club meetings and going to workshops.

I applied to internships, over one hundred of them, with my freshly made resume. I heard back from one and it was to let me know they wouldn't be moving forward. I had no clue what was going on. I revised my resume and applied to a few dozen more. I heard back from a few of those applications. I got dressed up and went to my interviews. Nothing. I had never experienced a professional interview, I wasn't even prepared for the handshake with the interviewer. I went back and did some research and realized my mistakes. I kept applying and finally landed an internship. Getting an internship was so important for me, because it was a step closer to possibly getting a full-time offer upon graduation.

One of the major changes in my life at this point was not that I went to DePaul or joined a certain club; it was that I started doing things for me and not for anyone else. I realized that for a long time I was trying to live up to a standard that I thought people had for me. I began doing things that I enjoyed and learned to take ownership of my life. Overall, I became a better human being by understanding that those "bad" moments are the ones that can shape us into someone stronger and wiser. Growing up, I blamed my surroundings for my unwillingness to grow, when in reality it was me who did not allow growth or success to manifest.

A couple months later, I began interning at the United States District Court for the Northern District of Illinois. I felt so honored to have the opportunity to be working at the courthouse. I finally felt I was on the right path. During that internship I started applying to more internships, and became more proactive about my career. I began looking for more opportunities by attending more career fairs and networking with more professionals.

I heard back from one, The Art Institute of Chicago. They had an accounting and finance internship for the summer of 2019, and I got the offer. At first, I wasn't sure if I should take it because it was a long commute from my house. However, I decided to accept and I loved it. I met phenomenal people. Even though it was a lot of work, I learned a lot about work ethics, professionalism, and responsibilities.

Everything started falling into place. I began landing more of the internships I was applying to and landed internships at Fortune 500 companies. All that hard work started paying off. I reached a point in life where things started to make sense. It wasn't because I landed jobs, but because I was in a better place with myself. I stopped blaming people around me for things that made me unhappy and took responsibility and action.

As graduation approached, I felt uneasy. I had been in school my entire life, and to see the end approaching was daunting. I had always been afraid to fail or to disappoint those around me, but the moment I began to change that mindset, things fell into place. I met people who constantly supported me. I became a better listener and friend. I began giving, instead of only receiving. It became important to me to learn a lesson from each opportunity

I encountered. I was exposed to many different personalities, but each one taught me something new.

I graduated from DePaul University in November of 2020 with a bachelor of science in business, with a major in economics. I signed a full-time offer with a Big Four accounting firm during the Covid-19 pandemic, and began my role in January of 2021. I learned that at the end of the day everything happens for a reason, and the important part is taking the good from every situation we encounter. I have learned a valuable lesson from every experience and to take chances, which ultimately shaped me into the person I am today.

THINK YOUNG AND GROW

I challenge you to think about the areas in your life in which you are not challenging yourself. Think about why you are not challenging yourself, and if it is attached to a fear of failure, rejection, etc. Once you are honest with yourself, you should push yourself outside of that comfort zone and grow. Begin taking chances and stop settling for what is comfortable.

I learned to strive to be a better version of myself every day, and that has resulted in opportunities that would have never presented themselves otherwise. By you taking the time to read this book, there is some intention on your behalf to grow already, but that does not end with you reading this book. That transpires into you pushing yourself to do things that require courage. This is easier said than done, but these actions are defining moments. Don't let fear stop you from growing.

THIS IS ME

My name is Yaritza Vallejo and I am young professional, rising entrepreneur, scholar, and emerging leader from Chicago, IL. Throughout my professional experience, I have developed strong critical thinking, organizational, and creative skills. With this, I have expanded my research ability through previous internships and growing professionally with every experience encountered.

My interests include mentorship, tech, consulting, and writing. I am a rising entrepreneur serving as co-founder of Latinas Becoming, a growing brand built on the foundation of empowering young Latina professionals who are making an impact. It is our mission to build a community reinforced by authentic connection, to help you discover the power within yourself.

THE TEN-YEAR PLAN

1. Earn a graduate degree, such as an MBA or JD after a few years of work experience
2. Travel to at least one country in every continent before I turn 30
3. Start an entrepreneurial venture

Jacqueline S. Ruiz

BIOGRAPHY

Jacqueline Camacho is a visionary social entrepreneur that has created an enterprise of inspiration. Her keen sense of service coupled with the vision to bring good to the world have led her to create two successful award-winning companies, establish two nonprofit organizations, publish 19 books, create over 10 products, and has held dozens of events around the world in just the past decade.

She is often referred to as a "dream catcher" as her strategies have supported thousands of women, authors and young ladies to live a life of significance. Jacqueline's quest to be a servant leader extends to every area of her life. She has shared her inspiration in four continents and aligned with some of the most powerful brands to elevate others. At only 37 years of age, she has achieved what most would not do in an entire lifetime. Being a cancer survivor sparked a sense of urgency to serve and transcend.

Jacqueline believes that magix (yes, a made-up word that means magic x 10) is the interception of profit and impact. She is one of the few Latina sports airplane pilots in the United States and is about to embark on the historic air race that 20 women flyers participated in crossing the United States 91 years ago, including the famous Amelia Earhart.

Jacqueline believes that *"taking off is optional, landing on your dreams is mandatory."*

Alexandria Rios Taylor

BIOGRAPHY

Alexandria Rios Taylor is a high school Assistant Principal in the southwest suburbs of Chicago. She works with youth on leadership development and career pathways. She delivers presentations which draw upon her personal experience in public education as well as research from her doctoral fieldwork. Her commitment to educational equity has served as the foundation for her conferences, workshops, and addresses. Alex is proud to be partnering with Jackie on this collaboration and is excited to be featured in the *Today's Inspired Latina series.*

Alex is currently pursuing her doctorate degree in educational administration at Aurora University as she examines the pipeline of diverse educators. She holds a master's degree in leadership and administration from Benedictine University and completed her undergraduate studies at North Central College. She double majored and earned a bachelor's degree in both organizational communication and Spanish where she received the Carleen Verstraete Award and the Rasmussen Scholarship. Alex was later recognized by her alma mater and received the Sesquicentennial Award in education as a top educator in her decade.

Although she is proud of her tenure as an educator and service to her community, nothing gives Alex more gratification than coming home to her two kids, Elena and Maceo, and her devoted husband, Gentri.

Made in the USA
Middletown, DE
24 June 2021

41867221R00141